THE CHILD.

THE CHILD:

BY

MONSEIGNEUR DUPANLOUP,

BISHOP OF ORLEANS.

TRANSLATED, WITH THE AUTHOR'S PERMISSION,

BY

KATE ANDERSON.

BOSTON:
PATRICK DONAHOE,
23, 25, AND 27, BOYLSTON ST.
1875.

Electrotyped by Jas. L. Duffy & Co.,
Pilot Job Press.

AUTHORIZATION.

25 Fév., 1873.

St. Hyeres,

Var.

Madame,

Je suis fort touché de la bonne lettre que vous avez bien voulu m'écrire, et je consens bien volontiers à ce que vous me demandez.

Je vous bénis bien paternellement en Notre Seigneur.

✠ F. Eveque d'Orleans.

TRANSLATOR'S PREFACE.

Being desirous that all Parents and Teachers in my country should have the advantage of the high theory, and the useful and practical instructions, respecting the education of the Child, contained in this Treatise, I have ventured on translating it. If my close adherence to the text be not consistent with what critics designate pure and classical English, I trust the beauty and sublimity of this great Bishop's language will be considered sufficient excuse.

I have the honor to remain,

The Translator.

AUTHOR'S PREFACE.

HAVING, after long study and laborious experience, sought, by the most profound reflection, to discover what the two fundamental rules in education were, I have found them to be authority and respect. For this reason, I consider I ought to place these two words, so important, before all, and commence with them. No doubt, the first pages of my book will not suffice to demonstrate what I advance here; it is the entire book which proves the demonstration. I venture to say there is not a page in which this truth, with its forcible and vivid light, is not repeatedly met. I do not doubt, even, that the penetrating glance of elevated and attentive minds will, from the first, discover why the two holiest and greatest sentiments which can exist in humanity on earth, to wit, authority and respect, are the greatest essentials in education, and appear as the foundation, and even the chief means of the work which it aims to accomplish. What is education actually? what is, at the same time, the highest, the most profound, the most general, the most simple conception of it? It is this: to cultivate, to train, to develop, to strengthen, and to polish all the physical, intellectual, moral, and religious faculties which constitute nature and human dignity in the child; to give to these faculties their perfect integrity; to establish them in the plenitude of their power and their action. Hence, to form man, and prepare him to serve his country in the various social offices he may some day, during his life on earth, be called on to fill; and thus, in a higher conception, prepare him for eternal life, by elevating his present life. Such is the work — such is the end of education. Such is the duty of parents, when God, uniting them by His supreme providence, gives through them life to noble creatures, and charges them with continuing and completing this entirely Divine task, of conducting to happiness, by truth and virtue, these children, whom he will, one day, associate with Himself in His eternal felicity and glory. Such is the duty of men who unite an honorable choice, a superior vocation, a generous devotion, to authority and parental solicitude; such is the holy mission of teachers of youth; and that always and everywhere, among the most learned and civilized nations, as well as the least enlightened and least polished peoples. Private education and public education, the most ordinary as well as the highest, the education of girls and of boys — in a word, human education — succeeds only on these conditions, and at this price. Otherwise it is not education. Such is the law of nature, and the order imposed by Providence itself. What is actually in question? It is important to understand it well from the first. Here is a child:

it is necessary to bring him up; but what does that mean, and what is this child? This child is mankind; he is entire humanity; he is man: nothing more, nothing less. He has a right to the solicitude of all the authorities, to the action and benevolence of all the powers on earth. He has a right to every respect, and he, in his turn, owes it to them. All the authorities, divine and human — the Prince, the Priest, the Teacher, the Magistrate, the Church, home and society, have been instituted for him. Moral discipline, instruction, literature, science, religion, all the prizes of labor and virtue; in fine, Providence and everything on earth exists for him; because he himself is on earth from God and for God! For this reason, all in this world ought to labor for his education; all ought to concur in bringing him up; all ought to perform or assist in this great work. With regard to the rest, the beautiful classical term, which is the foundation of the language adopted by mankind to designate education, suffices to point out that this is not a high and foolish theory, a magnificent speculation without possible reality. Indeed, the simple enunciation of these terms carries with it the clearness of real truth; and, in order to obtain the highest evidence of this, it will be sufficient to determine the ordinary and incontestable meaning of each expression; and to prove the nobleness, the elevation, and practical force of the general conceptions revealed by human language with respect to education. Let us now enter into details.

Take the word "education." What noble ideas, what powerful action, its etymology expresses here!

It is almost to draw out of nothing, almost to create; it is, at least, to draw the slumbering faculties out of lethargy and torpor; it is to give life, movement, and power to the still imperfect existence. It is in this sense that intellectual, moral, and religious education is the highest human work that can be performed. It is the continuation of the Divine work in that which is most noble and elevated — the creation of minds. And, for this reason, it is also the work of the highest authority.

In education, God is the source and ground of authority and respect; of the essential duties and rights of all: He is the model and image of the work which is to be performed; He is the most powerful and skilled workman in it. From whatever point of view I place myself in order to consider the work of education, it appears to my eyes as one of the most admirable reflections of the Divine power, wisdom, and goodness.

Education receives the foundation, the matter, which the first creation confides to it; it undertakes to form it; it imprints it with beauty, elevation, politeness, greatness; it is as an inspiration of life, power, grace, and enlightenment. When the immortal Archbishop of Cambrai undertook the education of the Duke of Burgundy, he applied himself, says the historian, and succeeded, in as much as was in his power, in forming and realizing in his royal pupil the perfection of virtue — as the artists of antiquity sought to impress on their works that supreme beauty which gives to human forms a supernatural and heavenly expression. It has been also said that the Duke of Burgundy was one of the noblest creations of wisdom and genius.

It is to the Romans — it is to their tongue, so sublime and so forcible, that we owe this word, so grave in meaning, so energetic in expression. The French have enriched the language, and even expressed the action of education, by a word, the nobleness and brilliancy of which contests with the sublimity and energy of the Latin word. Their expression is "*élever*" — to raise up, to elevate. Beautiful word! and, if the meaning proper to it seems less profound, and expresses less forcibly the action — the creative power of education, it adds to this fundamental conception, beauty, ornament, and greatness. And is the creative action of education really anything else? Yes; "*élever*" is a beautiful word, thoroughly French: it has dignity and greatness. It surrounds education with a natural *cortége* of the beautiful ideas which are attached to it. To elevate the soul; to elevate the mind; to elevate the sentiments and the thoughts; to elevate the character — are the natural conceptions of a nation, the duties and the end of education.

The merit due to France is that of having promptly understood all this, and worthily lent herself to it; the glory of French genius is that of having, on finding this language suited to it, instinctively adopted it; and then an education expressed and carried on so ought to be of the highest. Germany and England have not had the same inspiration, and they envy us; for it is one of these expressions which do honor to a nation; and, applied to education, it points out all the fecundity and power that exist in a word; and how it can pick up, in passing, noble and useful meanings, which, without it, would have remained unperceived and in obscurity. It is one of those words which not only enrich the language of a people, but enrich and strengthen their morals, and elevate a conception to its highest power. And when this conception is that of the education even of youth; besides, when this language has given to the world the expressions *genius* and *character*, two words still so French, and which are found, for the first time, with the elegance of their absolute meaning, in our national dictionary, is it not sufficient to justify me, if I permit myself to say that our tongue possesses, in its generous energy, some of those happy words, inspired from on high, which will ever be the property of France?

Education, then, forms, elevates, in some manner creates. It is in order to succeed in this, that it cultivates, it trains, it acts, and causes to act. For this reason, it is a work of high authority, and, at the same time, claims from those whom it brings up a respectful docility. It cultivates by physical cares, by intellectual instruction, by moral discipline, by religious lessons. Like an intelligent gardener, it places the plant which is confided to it in good earth; it waters it from a pure stream, surrounds it with generous food, and thus nourishes juices, which, in seconding the interior labor, assist active vegetation, and cause growth, in order to give flowers and fruit in the proper time. Education, then, cultivates, and this is especially the duty of the teacher. But that is not all. Education trains, and causes to act; it requires the active concurrence, the docile concurrence, the free, spontaneous, personal exercise, of the pupil. As the master of a young and noble courser makes him fly through space, ascend hills, draw burdens, struggle against fatigue, and thus gives to him all the suppleness, all the vigor, which he is capable of; in like manner, the teacher, in proposing certain studies, certain efforts, certain exercises to his pupil, in energetically inciting him, wisely directing him to them, causes him, as is suitable, to labor and efficaciously contribute, himself, to his own education. I have said, *as is suitable;* I should have said, as is necessary; for such is the design of God, and even of His providence. The child is a moral being, endowed with liberty, and capable of action; it is necessary that he should labor to develop, to ennoble, to elevate himself of himself; otherwise his education is not accomplished. The law of labor is the great law of human education. No one on earth is created in order to do nothing. Every intelligent and free creature is essentially destined to action. Activity nourishes, trains, gives strength and life. Idleness, or doing nothing, is annihilation — is death. I do not fear to declare, also, that the principal talent of the teacher consists in making his pupil enter courageously into the path of labor and personal application. Labor, or the exercise of the body, which gives vigor to its members; labor of the mind, which forms in it judgment, taste, reasoning, memory, imagination; labor of the heart, of the will, of the conscience, which forms the character, gives birth to modest tendencies and virtuous habits. Work of the master, and labor of the pupil.

Education is, then, at the same time, culture and exercise, instruction and study; the master cultivates, instructs, labors outwardly; but it is essentially necessary that there should be exercise, application, labor, within. It is indispensable to understand this well. In education, what the teacher does himself is a trifling matter; what he causes to be done is everything. Whosoever does not understand that, understands nothing of the work of human education. Education, from whatsoever side we consider it, is, then, essentially an action, and a creative action; the teacher and the pupil both essentially take part in it: the teacher, with authority and devotion; the pupil, with docility and respect. To the first belongs this powerful and fertile action respecting the child, this real authority, which gives him the right and imposes on him the duty of acting as master. In education, as elsewhere, without real authority there can be no legitimate action. But this action is an action entirely beneficent; for education is essentially a paternal service; the master replaces and represents a father.

In the teacher, devotion should inspire and encourage his action; kindness, affection, tenderness, should be the foundation and the soul of his devotion. In the pupil there should be profound docility, courageous efforts, grateful and inviolable respect towards an action which is a benefit; for an authority inspired by affection and devotion.

I have spoken of God, the parents, the teacher, the

child; I ought to speak of *school-fellows.* School-fellow; that is to say, the begining of society; social life, its duties and its rights; the noble emulation; the force of example; the sharing of joys and sorrows, labors and success; the artless friendships, the support, the mutual assistance, the fraternity even; for the school-fellow is the brother, the family, when education is what it ought to be. With school-fellows there will be reciprocal clashing, and, consequently, the beneficial teaching of mutual endurance and patience, true and wise equality, respect for others — all such precious sentiments. There are no, or very few, good educations without school-fellows.

Such are the chief conceptions; such are the rights and higher order of duties revealed by these first words: — TO CULTIVATE, TO TRAIN.

We shall now ascertain why we have said that education is, above all, a work of authority and respect.

CONTENTS.

THE CHILD.

CHAPTER I.

THE CHILD; HIS DISPOSITIONS, HIS FAULTS, HIS RESOURCES.

To cultivate, to train, to develop, to strengthen, and to polish all the faculties — physical, intellectual, moral, and religious — which constitute in the child nature and human dignity: such is the work of education.

The child is, then, the personal subject of education. It is important to study him to the heart, and to see closely what greatness he has in him, what resources he offers, and in the name of what noble qualities, in the name of what superior faculties, he claims the highest, the most tender solicitude, and all the cares of a religious respect. Should this book fall into the hands of those whom I have had the happiness to bring up, they will not be surprised at my language. Doubtless, in the days of their education, I spoke more frequently to them of my tenderness than of my respect. Nevertheless, I did not fear to disclose to themselves the secret of most delicate duties towards their soul; I loved to explain to them the devotion and respect with which the pious teachers of their youth believed they were bound to rear them. These dear children understood those lessons; and it is a homage which is to me as sweet to render as it can be glorious to them to receive; they have always shown themselves worthy of being pupils in the school of respect. But what, then, is the child that he should be deserving of a religious respect? The child: he is man himself, with all his future contained in his early years. The child: he is the hope of the family and of society; he is the human race springing up again; the country which perpetuates itself, and is as the renewing of humanity in its bloom. The child is an amiable creature, whose candor, artless simplicity, confiding docility, win affection and give birth to the most pleasing anticipations; he is the blessing of God and the depositary of heaven — an innocent soul, the peaceful sleep of whose passions has not yet been disturbed, whose uprightness has not yet been impaired by the fascinations of lying and the deceits of the world. The child is a simple and pure heart, to which Religion may present herself with confidence, which, as yet, has no private interests to prefer to her, and which willingly permits itself to be softened by her maternal voice. He is this first age of life, so sweet to see; so amiable to cultivate; most frequently so suitable to train; so easy to mould to the holiest duties; and always so interesting to study closely. Ah! I understand how childhood can have been so dear to the GOD OF THE GOSPEL. All in it breathes of innocence and grace. There is in this first age something which comes more recently from heaven, which calls forth all the blessings of the Divine Hand, and depicts to us on earth the sweetest charms of candor and virtue. You will say to me, perhaps, it is evident you take pleasure in speaking here of those children of benediction, who are innocence, docility, and wisdom itself; whom nature and grace seem to have vied in forming, and who appear to be born for the love of heaven and the delight of earth. No; I speak here of all children, whatever they may be. I take this age in its widest meaning; and I say that there is in it a grace, a dignity, a nobleness, which belongs to it; there is something of blessedness which breathes forth its celestial origin, and which is not in the generality of men. Nothing has yet been blighted or debased in this child, such as I represent him to myself. He has never committed an unworthy act with reflection; he has not yet lied with cleverness; he has not knowingly despised or hated virtue — justice, natural equity, and plain-dealing are quick in him. No doubt he bears in him, caused by the original stain, that inclination to evil which is now the sad inheritance of our nature; but it is a germ hidden in the depths of his soul, which has not yet received any development. No one is better acquainted with the faults of the first age than I, and I will presently show that I have neither any wish nor any need to ignore them. The long years which I have devoted to the care of children have been the sweetest, but also the most laborious, of my life; and if my hair has blanched before its time, it is in the service of childhood. Who elsewhere occupied with children has not met, does not know all there is in them to reform and correct by education. It is also, I say it without trouble, it is also in this age one meets side by side with the happiest dispositions, the most depraved instincts — stubbornness, passion, jealousy, lying — I will say even ingratitude. It is especially at this age egotism, thoughtless as it is, shows itself, prejudiced, capricious, and eager. I have never met with more profound selfishness than among children. When their early years have been cherished in effeminacy, with what secret repugnance they repulse all truth which wounds them! — with what deplorable instinct they seize all that is false or evil, and which flatters them! It is, above all, an inquisitive, unsteady, restless age — greedy of possession, enemy of constraint. It is this age which opens the eyes, with such dangerous eagerness, on life, to discover in it every charm; this age whose glances wander with anxiety on the smiling scene of the world, to see in it deceitful beauties — in fine, the age in which the heart, though still so young, awakens and glows for the first time at all which surrounds it, soliciting with ardor the food which is necessary for its desires, and hastening to taste the vain pleasures which perhaps will soon tarnish its innocence. I admit all that — why should I feign not to know it? It is precisely the inexperience, the weakness, the innumerable perils, and, above all, the faults, of this first age, which interest my heart, alarm my tenderness, and which claim from indifference itself solicitude and paternal cares. I repeat, then, childhood is giddy, inattentive, presumptuous, violent, stubborn; it is the age of heedlessness, waywardness, and pleasure; the age of all the illusions, and hence almost all the errors, of this age, and also all the laborious cares of education. "But," added Fénelon, "it is the only age in which man can count on himself to correct his faults;" and, I ask, what is more winning, and, I will add, more worthy of respect, than a being so young making efforts to become better? Is it not one of the most glorious and most moving privileges of childhood? Mature age, and especially old age, are almost without resources against their faults; they can only with great difficulty reclaim themselves from the unfortunate bent they have taken, and extirpate the evil which has grown old with them. There usually remains to them but a constitution weakened and spoiled by custom. As to children, if they, like men, have *faults of disposition,* they have not, at least yet, those *acquired faults* which the progress of time, the influence of habit, and the fatal strength of nature, fully developed for evil, caused to be justly designated vices. All is still pliant in them, and all is new; it is easy to set straight again these tender plants and raise them towards heaven. Nothing is worn out, nothing is deeply rooted, in these young and capricious creatures.

There is nothing more lovely to see, even in the midst of these faults, than the dawning reason and virtue of a child — "lilium inter spinas," say the Scriptures; nothing more touching to observe than the first efforts he makes against himself, to correct himself. How necessary to exhort and sustain him then; with what affection he must be made to comprehend that one blesses God for his courage; he must be made to feel that one is happy by it. It is very necessary to convince him of it, and one can never give too much tender encouragement to a child who labors to conquer his temper and control himself, who is sensible of his faults, reproaches himself with them, acknowledges them candidly, loves those who reprehend him, and, in good time, puts his hand to the great work of his own improvement. We cannot, then, be too careful; for we often deceive ourselves. Yes; too frequently we become terrified without reason at the faults of early youth. Under the most rugged bark there is sometimes a stock living and full of sap, which will give excellent fruits: so also a mild and polished exterior sometimes conceals a deceitful heart and the wretched principles of corruption. It is especially necessary to distrust those who are spoken of as fine children. I do not say we should be prejudiced against them; but it is necessary to look well to them; they rarely become that which they promise. On the contrary, notwithstanding the appearances of giddiness and too lively an inclination for pleasure, a child may be wise, reasonable, and sensible to virtue. I have many times met with these young beings, who, under the turbulent exterior of their age, concealed a reason already much matured, a clear mind, a firm, decided character, even in the midst of the mobility of their impressions, and I avow these were the children who interested me most; that it was with them I had need to guard against the preferences of my heart. I do not, then, make any difficulty in acknowledging it. The child, even he who at his birth has received from heaven the happiest disposition, is a weak, fickle being, who wanders from desire to desire, at the mercy of his own inconstancy. It seems as if nothing can fix him; that he is incapable of applying his mind to anything — of forming a resolution, of taking a serious part; in everything he appears to follow fancy, the most frivolous whims, and to have nothing steady; all in eternal agitation. But religious instructors may permit me to say in their name, it is the work and even the glory of education to conquer this fickleness and settle this unsteadiness; it is also the work and the glory of youth.

I have helped to this triumph, and I have enjoyed it. I have seen children, before their twelfth year, faithful at the hours of silence, attentive to the lessons of knowledge and virtue, eager to labor, ardent in the struggles of emulation, re-collected at prayer, and I have said to myself: what pure joy! what honor for those who brought up those children, and who have contrived to form minds so mature, hearts so firm, souls so thoughtful, in so early an age! How impossible not to love children — so courageous and so amiable! What happiness to expend one's love and cares in forming them! How impossible not to admire a childhood so noble and so pure — so generous and so docile! Pardon me my prepossessions for this age; but I should admit I attach great importance to convincing the teachers of youth that the natural faults, even the faults which frighten them most, ought to inspire their zeal, their affection, I will almost say their respect, for childhood. Let them regard it closely, and they will see that the most turbulent, the most restless child, has, in the midst of all his faults, something true, ingenuous, and natural, which is of infinite value, and merits every respect. In more advanced age, alas! our good qualities have refinements which alter them: he, the child, is naturally upright and sincere; as yet he has nothing put on — nothing factitious; it is true he sometimes appears too much without restraint, and this is complained of. As for me, I hardly complained of it; because I found him almost always without affected reserve, without envy, and, notwithstanding his natural egotism, without anxious or skilful reverting to himself — without interested pre-occupation. Simple and easy, free in his career, the child pauses not to compose himself with art; and in these precious moments, when he likes to settle himself near you, to listen to you with attention, you would be surprised to see that which I have seen a thousand times — how worthy he is of the sweetest, the most intimate familiarity; how deeply your culture has penetrated into that young soil; with what facility the way is found to his heart, to engrave there rapidly the most profound impressions.

Yes; the giddiest child, I would almost say the most violent, is that same who suddenly shows, to those who know how to make him love them, a taste for candor and truth which enraptures; it is he who suddenly causes to be perceived in his heart, when we have discovered how to soften it, I cannot tell how much of sweet, innocent, gentle merriment, which moves us profoundly. I persist in maintaining this opinion: whatever may be the harshness of his character and the violence of his temper, when a child is without meanness, when he has uprightness, courage, a heart truly sensitive, and a feeling of religion, it is not necessary to be anxious about him. Fénelon speaks somewhere of a child who was confided to him for some time, and who, though still very young, had wit, boldness, and facility for speaking; but a character strong even to hardness, very quick passions, violent whims, an impetuous temper, and his reason not yet sufficiently strong to restrain him. Once carried away he never recollected himself; one could not contrive even to make him perceive the wrong. He hardened himself coolly, and despised correction. But it was all these faults which gave Fénelon great hopes for the future of this child: "His faults," said he, "come from his temperament and his age. There is every ground for believing that good education and more matured reason will convert them into true talents. He is a wine whose sharpness changes, mellows with age. He has a very strong character; it is but a question of softening it. Age, which matures reason, example, instruction, authority, will temper this childish impetuosity. Much mildness, patience, and firmness is necessary. He must be led with a mild, patient, and uniform firmness. There is a depth of sense and strength in him from which much may be expected, provided he be accustomed gradually to restrain himself; this child will then have many profitable qualities."[1] Beyond dispute, Fénelon reveals here one of the most profound secrets of human nature and Christian ethics, also the most important to be well understood by those devoted to the education of youth. The liveliest, the strongest, and the happiest characters are not, indeed, those without faults, without passions, and without struggles. Who has not heard of the struggles and victories of St. Paul, St. Augustine, St. Teresa, St. Jerome, St. Francis Xavier, and so many others? There has never been question of bringing up children without passions and faults: I would almost venture to say, nothing could be worse than such children — nothing more problematical than the success of their education. As to me, I foresaw it always, and was accustomed to say of them — "These are sleeping and deceitful waters: there will come to us from them more of evil than good!"

A thousand times better those lively, impetuous, passionate natures. No doubt they require to be strongly governed; but they likewise offer great re-

[1] Fénelon loved children. At sixty-four years of age he charged himself with superintending, in his palace at Cambrai, during an autumn, the education of the young sons of the Duke de Choulnes; he spoke of them with tenderness. "Forget not," he wrote to their father, "that you have promised me the dear young folk for the fine season. I will be charmed with them." Another time: "I ask of you your dear children, who are mine." They will not embarrass me in any way; I will be charmed with them, and will be their first tutor under M. Gallet. Leave me the little folk; they will give me pleasure; I will try not to be useless to them." Another time he wrote to their mother: — "As to the little flock, I am charmed to have them here; I love them tenderly. They will not encumber me in any way."

sources for great things. What do the masters of ethics understand by the passions? They understand those powerful impulses, those impetuous movements of the soul, which drive it to love and to hate. To what have they compared them? To generous coursers, which transport and precipitate the soul into the extremes of good or evil, according as a firm or a lax hand takes possession of the reins. Thus, though children be ardent, headstrong, and fiery; though they may have a lively imagination, a mind haughty at times, an irritable temper, an excessive sensibility, I do not feel alarmed for their education; these, at least, will not languish in mediocrity, without faults, without reproaches, but also without virtue. I ask for them but a hand capable of seizing the reins, and cleverly directing their strong and generous natures. The children who gave me most trouble had at bottom an excellent heart, an elevated mind, a noble soul. I found them always true, sensible, sincere; there were usually the most grateful of all, and at heart the most docile; they accustomed themselves most courageously to obedience, to labor, to the love of letters, and respect for their masters; always more prompt to enthusiasm for good than to resentment for evil; and when, at length, the happy disposition which was in them triumphing, by the grace of God and their education, over the faults and weaknesses of their age, strengthened itself in wisdom and virtue, they became, in reality, those youths who promise at twenty to be the most amiable and generous of men.[1]

[1] Rousseau.

CHAPTER II.

THE CHILD; MY EXPERIENCES.

In order to improve children, not to be disheartened by their faults, and to discover all their qualities, it is necessary to love them, and to feel the happiness of being loved by them; to be interested in them; to show joy at seeing them near us; to study them with intelligence and love; and to take pleasure in chatting familiarly with them. In such conversations their tempers become softened and restrained. All haughtiness, all harshness, disappears; they are not only polite, sociable, complaisant, sincere, playful, grateful, and tender, but their minds become elevated, their hearts open, and we discover in them the most touching traits. Their souls entirely expand, and we sometimes suddenly perceive behind this sweet, smiling little face, and in the heart of this restless creature, a something great and divine, which at first surprises, but which we soon venerate with tenderness. Fénelon, when speaking of this wonderful grace called simplicity, adds that it is the evangelical pearl, worthy of being sought in the most distant lands. It is a diamond of so pure a water that it reflects the most brilliant lights! The shores of the Ganges, which send to us the pearls of the East, have not sent us simplicity; yet I have found it in the heart of a child. No doubt the candor of their mien, the vivacity of their looks; this color so pure, this smile so gracious; these words so artless and so amiable; all the innocent beauties and exterior charms of this age possess a great power; but the charms of the heart are still more powerful. See how this simplicity unknowingly inspires the child with the highest virtues. We can say of him what the apostle says of charity: he believes all; he hopes in all; he seeks all that is amiable and good; he admires all that is noble and great; he suspects no evil; he grieves not for wealth; he enjoys himself with all that is innocently pleasant. You love him, he loves you; you appear virtuous, he venerates you. His actions are not dictated by ambition, malignity, bitterness, nor ill-will. At the recital of a generous action his heart beats, his eyes kindle. At the sight of misfortune his tears flow; he understands and divines the wants of misery; he waits not till they are exposed to him by some kind and eloquent tongue. His eye is the quickest to discover the poor man who tremblingly follows his steps; his hand is always the first to open for his relief. No; I am not surprised that Jesus Christ, when his disciples once disputed among themselves as to who should be the greatest in the kingdom of heaven, called unto Him a young child, and, having embraced him, placing him in the midst of the attentive crowd, said to them: "Verily I say unto you, If you become not like unto this little child, you shall not enter the kingdom of heaven." [1]

[1] St. Matthew, chap. xviii.

It can be seen that I do not recount here the dreams of my friendship for childhood and youth. For, since the days of Jesus Christ, who has desired to be the instructor and friend of this early age, what teacher, worthy of his divine mission, has not experienced that of which I am going to speak? Who has not sometimes seen, with profound emotion, in these young hearts, this ardor so beautiful, this docility so confiding, this generosity so courageous, these strong and lively inspirations, which well up from the innocent soul of youth; and, when the fitting time arrives, that sublime taste, that enthusiastic admiration for virtue and truth, suddenly engage them? Ah, how much they, who value childhood and youth so little, deceive themselves! Age pure and brilliant, noble and sincere! Heroic time of life! Admirable age! when a religious education inspires its affections, directs its efforts, sanctifies its ardor, restrains its passions, corrects its faults, foresees its errors, and embellishes its virtues. It is the age of the purest thoughts, the most generous affections, the most faithful friendships, and, on two occasions, especially, have I experienced it, of intrepid courage for good, and even, when necessary, magnanimous devotion. Behold the blessed privileges which render childhood and youth worthy of the most assiduous care and the tenderest love! it will always be with inexpressible consolation and warm regard that a religious instructor rests his eye on childhood, or recalls to his memory those virtues so genuine, and sometimes so strong; so artless and so simple of this early youth. Pardon me, if I indulge here in some personal recollections. To them I am indebted for the little authority attached to my words; to them I owe those sweet emotions of ancient friendship not yet extinguished in my soul, and which probably never will be, and on account of which I wish to return for a moment towards a past which to me is always present. During the pleasant and happy years of my life devoted to the cares of education, I loved to see the children who were confided to me. It was one of my pleasures to descend into their courts and gardens at the hours of their recreation, to join them, and sometimes take part in their amusements. Many of them may remember it. Or, if fatigue did not permit the agitation (frequently a little violent) of their plays, I loved to become a silent and tranquil spectator, and to walk peacefully among them, even in the midst of the bright effervescence of their gayest pastimes. I found there an inexpressible sweetness and peace. At times, when my ministry obliged me to mix with the world and its affairs, grieved by the sorrowful scenes of ever-changing life, I returned to the *Petit Seminaire* with a secret and profound satisfaction. Half-an-hour with my children dispelled all clouds from my brow. I forgot the world, its perplexities, its harrowing cares and sad mistakes. Sometimes, looking on from afar, the noise of their frolics, the bursts of their merriment, their artless disputes, their prompt reconciliations, the liveliness of their sallies, and even their joy to see me, though only a remote spectator, caused me joy; then, their increasing eagerness, when they found me a nearer witness; and judge if their raptures and success did not produce a sweet refreshment in my soul, for which I thanked God — asking of Him to continue to bless this loving, amiable, and faithful flock; this generation of opening promise; this precious deposit committed to my zeal and care; the best hope of religion and country. I have seen men of the world, honorably connected during many long years with all the principal affairs of their country, experience the same impressions at the sight of our children. I have seen them moved almost to tears, whilst they contemplated, under the cool shades of our house at Gentilly,[1] these numerous young folk, in gay and giddy swarms, dotted around, as thick and pleasant-looking as the flowers of the fields, tasting, through their innocent plays, such pure delight. I also loved to superintend their labors. How many times have I left my own occupations to surprise them at study! Yes; it was a noble sight to behold all those children collected, studious, and silent! — those two hundred young minds, intent on understanding, eager to penetrate and admire the great masterpieces of selected and varied literature. It delighted my eyes and my heart. But of this kind, nothing could equal the pleasure their examinations gave me. When I heard them recite with marked self-possession, explain with taste, interpret with fidelity, warmth, and enthusiasm, the finest pages of Virgil, Homer, Cicero, Titus Livius, Fénelon, and Bossuet, I felt profoundly happy. What could be more consol-

[1] A little village, one league from Paris, where the Petit Seminaire of St. Nicholas had a country-house.

ing for us than to see them thus happily sensible to the noble pleasures of intellectual culture and development? — their dawning reason instructing itself by the light of those wonderful minds, sometimes inspiring itself around the hearths of these great geniuses. I marvelled that the genius of Homer, of Virgil, of Bossuet, of St. John Chrysostom, should journey through centuries to form an alliance with those young minds, influence them, fructify and elevate them almost to the proud level of their own. If their pastimes and studies afforded me such pleasure, what shall I say of their piety? It can hardly be related. How delightful to see them collected in their pious sanctuary! What lively faith! What fervor in prayer! On our feast-days and those heavenly mornings, the remembrance of which they can never lose, the Angel of the Lord seemed really to welcome them, and shelter them under his sacred wing. It was on those blessed days, especially, that I liked to draw near and converse with them; to look closely into their hearts. It appeared to me that happiness, the peace of innocence, and all the perfumes of heaven, dwelt there. No doubt, the cares of the human state came in their time to trouble these joys of innocence and grace; but these light clouds of childhood once dispersed, I discovered in the depth of these young souls, as it were, a sky of azure, where God Himself caused to shine, in an horizon of infinite purity, lights of a divine splendor. It was then an amiable, a noble modesty; this virtue, which so profoundly ignores itself, enhanced and concealed all that they did. Their lightest discourse, their simplest words, had hidden ineffable graces, which it became hopeless to resist.

In those sweet and familiar conversations, how many times have I gleaned from the lips of childhood ideas of the most sublime simplicity! My tenderness for them was great; nevertheless, I could but imperfectly express to them the feelings of my heart; especially for those in whom I saw grace thus gradually transforming, softening, purifying, and ennobling nature. How many have there not been among them of whom I can say, that I recognized and loved in them God present and personified, under the most amiable exterior! Their childhood was that of the Saviour! like Him, they increased in age, in wisdom, and in grace before God and men. I have often asked myself, Whence comes this inexpressible charm of childhood and youth? Why has this early youth so much of grace that charms and softens, but never wearies? A friend whom I venerate, one day replied to me: "No doubt, childhood is simplicity, candor, innocence; but what adds to all this an undefinable, irresistible charm is, though the child is the joy of the present, he is especially the hope of the future!" These words struck me, and recalled those which were addressed to Louis XV. by a lady who was present at his consecration — she was the Marchioness de Pisieux: — "Ah, sire," said she, "it was you who should then be seen — you were beautiful; beautiful as hope!" It was saying all. A child-king could not receive more delicate praise — a finer lesson. But always, and whatever may be his condition, the child is the smiling, the beautiful, the sweet, the pure hope. The Holy Scriptures have lavished upon him the most gracious comparisons. The child is a tender shoot, a weak plant, it is true; but which will, perhaps, one day be a great tree, laden with all the fruits of virtue, and casting its glorious shadow afar. He is a flower ready to blow, and which promises a rich blossoming. If he appears already, in his first hour, so beautiful, what will he be when clothed with all the charms and embellished with all the gifts of heaven? he will rise up to adorn the earth. Again, the child is a weak brook, a newly-born spring; but he will, perhaps, become a majestic river. The teacher is the clever surveyor, of whom the Holy Book speaks: his hand directs those docile waters, guiding them where he pleases, and never permitting any strange, impure, or bitter waters to disturb their course. Yes; the child is the hope — the hope even of heaven; for he is the heir of the eternal palms, the object of God's complacency, the brother and the friend of the angels. He is the hope of the earth, of which he is already the riches and the treasure, and of which he will one day be the strength and glory. He is the hope of his country and of all humanity, which renews itself and grows young again in him. He is, especially, the hope of the family, of whom he is the joy and the delight, and of whom he will one day be the crown and the honor. Lovable creature! — his first appearance in the world, his first smile, his first look, is a sign of peace, an omen of serenity for all. Gaze on him: there is no cloud on his forehead; he ignores the past, he smiles at the present, he bounds towards the future, and seems to bear every one there with him. Sometimes I also ask myself: Why does he give so much pleasure to his oldest relatives? they never weary of looking at him, blessing him, listening to him, admiring his strength, his agility, his grace. The brightness, the sweetness of that smile, the transparency of that look, the limpidity of that countenance; no doubt all this reminds them that we grow old, that we wither, that we die every day; but also that we should neither wither, nor grow old, nor die: and the child is to them a remembrance, a reflection of that immortal youth which was the primitive inheritance of our nature. Nevertheless, I will say it, at the risk of repeating myself, the more I reflect upon it, the less I am surprised that the Son of God, in His passage on earth, should have loved children, and shown His joy in blessing them. Jesus Christ loved men, and He blessed them all in blessing childhood, which is the hope of the great human family. Who is not acquainted with the scenes of the Gospel? Our Lord, passing through the towns and cities, doing good, and healing the sick. The mothers, always so clever at divining the hearts worthy of them, hastening on His footsteps, leading to Him their little children, asking of Him to bless them. The children and the mothers were so numerous that the wearied apostles wished to send them away. But the Divine Master ordered that they should give place to them: "Suffer little children to come unto me," said He; "the kingdom of Heaven is for those who resemble them." Then taking these little children, He placed His hands on their heads, blessed them with tenderness, pressed them to His heart, and repeated: "Suffer little children to come unto me; the kingdom of Heaven is for those who resemble them." That was saying everything: the price of eternal life was revealed; the necessity of a regeneration and a new innocence was declared; and henceforth the gates of the kingdom of Heaven should remain firmly closed against whosoever refused to descend to that age. Even if the Son of God should have come from heaven to say this alone, it would suffice for His glory and the happiness of mankind. Who had said it before Him? who had thought and felt after this manner? During four thousand years — saving some cold words dropped from the minds of a philosopher — childhood had been the object of the contempt of sages and the cruel carelessness of legislators! But, in the midst of universal corruption, it was the dearest and the only love of heaven; and when the Father of the family came to seek again His children, when the Creator came to make Himself known to His own, it was not by pompous words He declared Himself. No; before showing Himself as the Master and Teacher of the world, it pleased Him to reveal Himself under a more touching aspect and a more tender name. They understood well the greatness and the power of the King of Heaven; but it was especially as a tender Father they understood, above all, His love; and when He said, "Suffer little children to come unto me, the Kingdom of Heaven is for those who resemble them," fathers and mothers, melted by it, prostrated themselves at His feet, and adored Him.

Ah! I understand why the prophets have exalted by such magnificent praises the glory of the patriarchs, and the noble pride of maternal fecundity! In concluding these lines, I will willingly cry out with them, and repeat the evangelical exclamation: "Blessed are the mothers whose wombs, holily fructified, have given to earth and heaven a numerous offspring!" "Blessed are the breasts which have suckled them!" Never has a mother placed more noble jewels on her bosom; never did a more beautiful crown encircle her glorious forehead!

CHAPTER III.

THE SPOILED CHILD.

THE spoiled child! I could have wished not to discourse on this painful subject; but I cannot avoid it, especially in a book which treats of authority and respect. The deadly enemy of authority and respect is the spoiled child. And, on the other hand, to spoil a child is to fail as sadly as possible in the respect that is due to the dignity of his nature, and the interest which his destiny and his honor claim. Persons at times laugh in speaking of spoiled children. I have never laughed at them; the sight of a spoiled child has never drawn from me a smile. Nothing is less pleasing. It is to me something frightful — frightful at the present, frightful in the future. Justice and truth often pierce through the levity of the words of men: he is an "enfant terrible," they say sometimes, with an agreeable carelessness, or even a certain satisfied vanity. Yes, terrible; and more so than they will some day wish him to be! for it is truly of the spoiled child that the words of Holy Scripture may be quoted: — "The whelp will become a lion, and will learn one day to devour men." (Ezechiel, xix. 6.) "What do you do all day?" said some one to a young wife. "I occupy myself in spoiling my children," she said.

That was, in her idea, but a sally more or less witty; but these words were more serious than she thought. By them she bitterly condemned the many imprudent mothers who seem, in a word, to have no other occupation but that of spoiling their children during the first part of their lives. She condemned herself bitterly. She knew it later, by cruel experience. "But the children are so young," they say; "what harm is there in spoiling them a little? It is of no consequence; it is only a matter of some years." No; it is for life. The Eternal Truth has pronounced the formal oracle on it—"The young man shall be in more advanced age that which they will have made him in his childhood." (Prov. xx. 6.)

There are many methods of spoiling a child: his mind may be spoiled by the thoughtless exaggeration of praise; his disposition may be spoiled by allowing him his own will in everything; his heart may be spoiled by occupying one's self to excess with him—adoring him, idolizing him. All these methods of spoiling children, this sad art of depraving an age which is the hope of an entire life, may be attributed to the development of those two fatal principles, the sources of all human perversity—effeminacy and pride. Nothing can give an idea of what children become who are spoiled by effeminacy; who are spoiled because too many caresses are bestowed on them; because too much tenderness is shown to them; because everything is granted to their tastes, their appetites, their looks, their idleness, and their wishes. They are sometimes truly little wild animals. They appear, and usually are, what are called pretty children; gracious and complaisant fawners. There is no insinuating little contrivance, no agreeable meanness, of which they do not possess the secret, in order to obtain what they desire from you: if you do not regard them closely, you find them charming; but if you suddenly perceive their cleverness and your own weakness; if you attempt resistance; if you require from them the least labor, the lightest application — immediately temper, angry and pouting silence, or even brutal and violent rudeness, reveal to you that these children — so amiable — are infant deceivers; that at heart and in truth, like tamed animals, they are sensible only to the bait by means of which they are tamed; that they become again wild and wicked, as soon as anything is refused to their appetites. Perhaps I exaggerate. Is this age, so tender, capable of so much wickedness? Here is what Fénelon and St. Augustine thought of it, and what they remark, in speaking of the earliest childhood: "Consider," said Fénelon, "how from this age children seek those who flatter them, and avoid those who try to control them; how well they know whether to cry or to be silent, in order to obtain what they wish for; how much they have already of artifice or jealousy." "I have seen," says St. Augustine, "a jealous infant! He could not yet speak, but with a pale face and angry eyes he looked at the child that sucked with him." Certainly I do not like dry, hard, and haughty children; but tender, insinuating, supple, caressing children, though more amiable at first sight, are, in my opinion, not less to be suspected, and incur the greatest danger in their education; and what adds to the peril is, we are easily taken by them. The cleverest are often deceived in them. "It is necessary to observe," says Fénelon, "that there are children whose dispositions deceive one greatly. They appear pleasing at first, because the early graces of childhood have a lustre which covers everything, and one sees in them something tender and amiable, which prevents us from examining closely and in detail the features of the face." And then what happens? One amuses himself with them; sometimes boasts of them; flatters them; and permits them to be flattered by every one, by little slaves, by servile women, who seek to insinuate themselves about them by mean and dangerous fawning, humoring all their whims, and nourishing, as if it were a pleasure, the most depraved of their little passions. Soon the deceitful graces of childhood vanish, the brightness becomes extinct, the tenderness of heart is lost; suddenly is discovered in them a desolating dryness, a profound depravity, and, in the end, these pleasing children become truly frightful; it is perceived then, but when too late, that there are no beings more hard, more wicked, more haughty, more violent, more egotistical, more ungrateful, more unjust, more odious, than children spoiled by effeminacy. Pardon me for dwelling on such painful details. Nothing has less charm for me. I do it only through compassion, through duty, through charity, in order to spare to parents, to families, to children themselves, the undoubted calamities which are the necessary consequences of the evil that I deplore. Weak and inconsiderate parents who play with the rising passions of their sons and their daughters, who seek but to divert themselves with them during their childhood, even to permitting them all kinds of excess, have not meditated on these things; have not foreseen all they will one day have to suffer from the licentiousness, the ingratitude, and the passions of these unfortunate children. Let them think of it, at least to-day, and allow me to call all their attention to this grave subject. The pagans themselves understood all the importance of it: "Above all," said an ancient philosopher, "above all, let the life of children be frugal, their clothing simple, and of the same kind as that of their school-fellows.[1] Do not permit them to fall

[1] Nothing is worse for children, spoils them more sadly and more quickly, than vanity in dress. It is necessary to inspire them at an early age with contempt for it. As for me, at the Petit Seminaire of Paris, I mercilessly banished all vain refinements of dress. For example, I never permitted the display of watches and gold chains. I said to them: "You shall wear a gold chain when you merit it. Be first in your class. It will then be a just and honorable distinction of genius, labor, and good conduct." Perfumes, and those who used them, I always condemned unmercifully. I said to them, and I repeated to them, when necessary, the saying of the ancients: "Hoc mihi suspectum est quod oles bene . . . non bene olet, qui bene semper olet." With respect to those who gave too much attention to their hair, I repeated bluntly that which a man of great experience said to me one day: "Be certain that a school-boy who combs himself with affectation, and looks after his cravat, becomes a bad scholar, and is most frequently on the eve of being disorderly in his behavior." Many may consider this severe; but it is the severity of experience. To return to the subject of watches and gold chains: I have never relished the religion of parents who promised vanities of this kind to their children, as rewards on the day of their first communion. The day of first communion requires no reward but itself. Besides, they are a real danger to the newly-born piety of those poor

into idleness and sloth. Remove all approaches to effeminacy: nothing disposes more to passion than a delicate and effeminate education. The indulgence granted to only sons, and the liberty which wards enjoy, are inevitable sources of corruption. What can become of a child to whom nothing has ever been refused, whose anxious mother has unceasingly dried his tears, and who has always been right in opposition to his masters? It is necessary to prevent children from being flattered. Let them hear the truth; let them sometimes understand fear, and always respect; let them have deference for their superiors, and never obtain any thing by anger. That which you refused them when they wept, grant them when they become calm." (Seneca, v. vii. p. 161.)[1]

children. I have sometimes seen the watch more adored than God Himself on this great day. Even religious and wise parents entertain strong illusions, when they imagine things relating to the soul can be dealt with by such means. I remember, among others, a very honest man, to whom I thought it my duty to complain of his son. He was a very giddy, indocile, turbulent child. I believed I ought to warn the father, even in presence of the child, that, if he did not soon make a serious and profound change, his first communion would be impossible. The father was greatly moved, but the child remained insensible. Then this excellent man began to weep; and seeing that the moment had come to spare nothing, in order to soften his son, and induce him to make an effort to improve, he turned towards him with a lively emotion, and said to him: "What trouble you give me! Well, listen, if you make your first communion, I will give you a horse." He was an old officer and a great sportsman. It can be well understood that his exhortation gave me but slender assistance.

[1] "Tenuis ante omnia victus, et non pretiosa vestis, et similis cultus cum æqualibus. In desidiam otiumque non resolvemus, et procul a contactu deliciarum retinebimus. Nihil enim magis facit iracundos quam educatio mollis et blanda. Ideo unicis quo plus indulgetur, pupillisque quo plus licet, corruptior animus est. Non resistet offen-

If I dwell on these sad remarks, I do it also through compassion for the teachers of youth, in order to spare them all that is most unthankful in their task. All these observations are the result of experiences and recollections: —

> "Non ignori mali miseris succurrere disco."

In the laborious functions of public education, I have never found anything more sorrowful to see, more painful to bring up, than spoiled children; and I should acknowledge that all my cares, all my efforts, for them, nearly always failed. I say it especially of children spoiled by effeminacy — these I have always found almost incurable. Children spoiled by pride sometimes gave us, during long years, the hardest labor; but, thanks to the spirit of emulation, to the devotion, the enlightenment of the masters, thanks to the skilled education which we imparted, we have often accomplished the end with time. Children spoiled by pride offer, without doubt, a sad spectacle, but at all times a spectacle less hideous than that of children spoiled by effeminacy. Thanks to the simplicity of his youth, the pride of a child can never deeply deprave all his fine and noble qualities. There are in these proud natures great resources for education; while in children spoiled by effeminacy there remains nothing but corruption, vice, a savage and a sensual egotism. In truth, it is intellectual,

sis, cui nihil unquam negatum est, cui lacrymas sollicita semper mater abstersit, cui de pedagogo satisfactum est. . . . Longe itaque ab assentatione pueritia removenda est: audia verum, et timeat interim, vereatur semper; majoribus assurgat, nihil per iracundiam exoret, quod flenti negatum est, quieto offeratur. . . ."

moral, and physical annihilation; nothing is sound in them but a depth of cowardly effeminacy, where every evil, every ignominy, every moral misery, springs naturally from the soil. In my compassion for them, I often compared them to young shrubs which a treacherous soil has nourished with poisoned juices; to tender flowers withered by mischievous winds, and whose natural perfume has become an odor of putrescence and death. To make the education of such a child, a new creation is necessary; it is necessary not only to correct but to remake nature. Prodigious undertaking! — there must be time, persistency, patience, firmness, an intelligence which is rarely to be met with in the required degree, and which would be even insufficient without extraordinary grace from God. The most merciful and the most powerful supernatural action only can accomplish the miracle of such a renovation. I would also have hope of it before the first communion; after it, never. Certainly it was by an entirely divine inspiration that the sage formerly pronounced these grave maxims, which I am happy to bring under the notice of parents. "He who loves his children never wearies of correcting them, hoping thence to find his happiness in them at the end of his days, and that he will never see them begging at the gate." (Ecclesiasticus, xxx. 1.) "You have children; give them a good education, and accustom them to the yoke of obedience from their tenderest years." (Id. vii. 25.) "It is not loving one's son to spare him chastisement: when one loves him truly, he applies himself to correct him." (Proverbs, viii. 24.) "Chastise your son without losing courage, lest he reduce you to the necessity of wishing him dead." (Id. xix. 18.) "The horse never accustomed to the bit becomes unmanageable, and the child abandoned to his caprices no longer knows the rein." (Ecclesiasticus, xxx. 8.) "Flatter your son, and he will cause you to tremble; play with him, and he will grieve you." (Id. xxx. 9.) "Be not too familiar with him, lest you soon have cause to repent of it, and that he at last reduce you to despair." (Ecclesiasticus, xxx. 10.) "Render him not master of his actions during his youth; watch him even to his thoughts." (Id. xxx. 11.) "Bow down his head and curb him in his youth: chastise him severely while still a child, lest he harden himself and wish no longer to obey you, and then he become the sorrow of your soul." (Id. xxx. 12.) "Instruct your son then; labor to form him, lest he dishonor you by a shameful life." (Id. xxx. 13.) "Permit not your son to live without discipline and rule." (Prov. xxiii. 13.) "If you bring him up with firmness, you deliver his soul from death." (Prov. xxiii. 14.) "Folly is, as it were, bound and tied up in the heart of a child; it is the rod of discipline that will drive it away." "Bring up your son well, and he will refresh your heart and delight your soul." (Prov. xxix. 17.) To these admirable maxims I will add only one observation, which justice claims in favor of one particular species of spoiled children — they are worthy of great compassion; and at all times how necessary to be guarded with respect to them! I speak of children spoiled on account of, or under pretext of, illness, weakness, or physical delicacy. The cares given to sickly children, lavished on them, and with which they are constantly surrounded, sometimes spoil these children in a deplorable manner. Nothing is more fatal to a child than to be during many years the tender and only object, constantly the object, of all the cares, of all the kind attentions, of all the pre-occupation, of a father, of a mother, and all the servants of the house. They know not how to deny him anything; the thoughts of all, the eyes of all, are unceasingly turned towards him; he is the centre of every tenderness. I repeat it, nothing is more worthy of compassion, because it is an evil almost unavoidable, and, nevertheless, a great evil; for many long years of good health and good education will be necessary to repair such a misfortune. It is well at least to be warned of the danger, and to avoid all that can be avoided. We should try not to give this dear little invalid useless attendance; to grant nothing but to a real want, with a wise kindness, a true solicitude. I have no hesitation in saying, that no education requires from a father or mother more wisdom, more foresight, more cleverness, more perspicuity, than the education of these poor children. I must now speak of children spoiled by pride. They have very often fine and gifted natures; but what dangers their education encounters! It is impossible to tell where their indocility, their impertinence, their vanity, their ostentation, their hardness, their naughtiness, their insolence, ever leads them. If education, instead of correcting in time these vicious dispositions, maintains and strengthens them, they will one day make their parents feel the weight of this pride, nourished with fatal complaisance. Alas! it must be acknowledged that it is most frequently the pride of the parents which excites, which develops, which gives birth to, the pride of the children. Fénelon formerly remarked this, and he thus traced the portrait of a child spoiled by pride: "His mother had nourished in him a naughtiness, a pride, which tarnished all that was most amiable in him. His disposition was good and sincere, but not winning; the thought of pleasing others scarcely entered his mind; he knew not how to grant with a noble and generous spirit; he appeared neither obliging, nor sensible to friendship; neither liberal nor grateful for the cares bestowed upon him, nor attentive to distinguish merit; he followed his fancy without reflection. The happiness of serving him was, in his opinion, sufficient recompense for those who waited on him. When there was question of pleasing him, nothing should be found impossible, and the least delay irritated his ardent temper. He had been flattered by his mother from his cradle, and he was a great example of the misfortune of those born in high station. The rigors of fortune, which he felt in his early youth, had not been able to restrain this impetuosity and naughtiness. His pride always rose again like the supple twig which re-elevates itself in spite of the efforts made to lower it." I cannot, then, too frequently repeat, whether it be to parents or to teachers: Take care; the more noble and more gifted the nature of the child you bring up, the more you should avoid depraving it by pride. If this noble nature has the determined disposition of this child, who might be a distinguished, and perhaps a superior man, you will make a tyrant, an odious being; he will look upon himself as different from the rest of men; it will seem to him that all others were placed on earth but to please and serve him, to anticipate all his wishes, to adore all his caprices, and address everything to him as to a divinity: like that Duke of Burgundy, of whom the Duke de Saint Simon tells us: "From the age of seven years he was hard-hearted, passionate, almost furiously so, towards inanimate things; frightfully impetuous; incapable of enduring the least resistance, even from time or the elements, without rushing into a rage which caused one to fear all in his body would burst; stubborn to excess; passionately attached to every pleasure and good cheer; madly to the chase; to music with a species of ravishment; again to play, in which he could not endure being vanquished, and where the danger with him was extreme — in fine, given up to every passion, and transported by every pleasure; often sullen, barbarous in raillery; striking the ridiculous with an accuracy which overpowered; regarding men, from the heights of his heaven, but as atoms, with whom he had no resemblance whatsoever." Behold what a bad early education had done for this child! of whom the education of the Archbishop of Cambrai afterwards made that admirable prince, whom even Voltaire praises, saying, "Under his reign France had been too happy." If this gifted nature, notwithstanding its talents, be vain and weak, your educating his pride will make of him a fool; a silly, vile, false being, speaking of everything at random, incapable of serious study, of eminent success; at most what is called a nice young man, that is to say, a cockscomb; useless to himself and every one else, and who often, if circumstances conduce to it, finishes at the age of twenty-five by dishonoring himself and his family. Fénelon, that great master in education, wished that this misfortune should be guarded against from the tenderest infancy, and, in order that children should not become what at present are called superb lions, instructs us not to make silly fools of them in the beginning. My readers will, I trust, judge kindly of me for bringing under their notice these observations, so delicate and so profound. "The amusement," said he, "which people wish to draw out of these pretty children often spoils them; they accustom them to hazard saying everything that comes into their minds, and to speak of things of which they have not yet a distinct knowledge; thus they acquire for life the habit of judging rashly, and speaking on subjects of which they have no clear ideas, which is a very evil disposition of mind. This amusement drawn from these children produces a still more pernicious effect—they perceive that they are regarded with complaisance, that everything they do is remarked, and that they are listened to with pleasure. Hence they accustom themselves to expect that every one will be always occupied with them. During this age, when they are applauded, and have not yet experienced contradiction, they conceive chimerical hopes, which lead to great disappointments during their lives. I have seen children who thought that every time people spoke in private they were speaking of them, because they observed it had been frequently done. They imagined there was nothing in themselves but what was extraordinary and admirable. It is necessary, then, to take care of children without letting them see that we think much of them. Point out to them that it is through friendship and the necessity of setting them right that you are attentive to their conduct, and not through admiration of their wit. Again, Fénelon said: "Whatever wit one finds in them surprises, because it is not expected at that age. All faults of judgment are permitted to them, and have the grace of ingenuity; people mistake a certain vivacity of body, which is never wanting in children, for that of mind. Hence it comes that the childhood which seemed to promise so much gives so little. Such a one was celebrated for his wit at five years of age, and sank into obscurity, and, in a measure, contempt, as he grew up." There is another species of little prodigies of whom it is necessary to be distrustful. Excuse what I am going to say, and be not surprised at it. Theirs is a case so delicate and so important that I cannot be silent on what I know and think of them. I speak of those little prodigies of wisdom and virtue, those children naturally correct and reserved, who always appear to have no faults, and grow up irreproachable. At the Petit Seminaire in Paris, I felt a hidden fear, as it were, an involuntary terror, every time a father or a mother brought their son to me, saying, "We have never had to reprimand him; he is truly a little perfection." I did not contradict them — it was hardly possible to do it then — but I said to myself, there is rugged work before me. I must have patience with the child and his parents. Perhaps I surprise you; but this surprise will cease when I add what remains to be said on this grave subject. Of all the observations which twenty-five years' experience in education has caused me to make, this is the most serious, the most profound, even the most sorrowful. I was frightened not only when parents led their son to me, saying, "We have never had to reprimand him;" but I was still more frightened, when, after many years of education at the Petit Seminaire, in spite of our care and our vigilance, we ourselves have never had to address a reprimand to a child. When we also said, "He is perfection;" and when charmed with such a work and such a success, we treated this child, this young man, as perfection. And what came to pass? Self-love grew in him, silently strengthened itself, and sometimes became gigantic and monstrous. The child was neither effeminate, nor vain, nor frivolous, nor weak. He had a serious mind, steady courage, and a sensible character. Frequently he possessed not only the taste, but the passion, for labor. This distinguished nature, watchful over itself, through conscientiousness and also the desire for praise, mixed with a subtle pride, had never to reproach himself; never was reprimanded by his masters; and avoided all faults, the greatest as well as the lightest; and, nevertheless, evil struck in him its deepest roots. The following observation accounts for one of the most grievous secrets of human nature: The homage which this habit of virtue attracts, even the peace which it gives, has its danger — it spoils the heart by too great a satisfaction with itself, which renders it most sensitive to everything that disturbs the interior peace, and, when mistakes occur, revolts, exasperates, and suddenly transforms mildness into passion, if the virtue be not solid, and has not been frequently tried by contradiction. Let us add, there is, perhaps, no virtue that does not cover some fault, which increases and strengthens under its shade and unknown to it, like those wild plants which shoot from the foot of a fine tree, and only appear dangerously bristling with thorns if the tree falls. I was many years before I understood the danger of these premature perfections; but when experience at length enlightened me, when I discovered the depths, and many times the abysses, of pride concealed in these gifted natures, it may be imagined that there were no children to whom I gave more care and attention. It was the ruin of our work in its most eminent success, the ruin of education in its noblest subjects, the overturning of the most beautiful edifice. I have no hesitation in saying there is something wanting in education when neither fault nor reproach is met with. How many times have I not said, in looking at and observing these, children, When can I make him a just reprimand, and pierce the wound which is forming in his soul — the wound which gnaws it, and which at the end of a certain number of years will have devoured all its good parts? But this operation must be performed at once with strength and tenderness; with strength, otherwise an invincible resistance is met with. Sheltered in an apparent respect, the child repulses all your warnings and all your lessons. His resistance is painted in his surprise, in the play of his countenance, in the colors which succeed each other on it, in a certain cold and wounded air, and even in his silence — the token of his offended dignity. It is then that rebellious pride mounts and roars in his heart like a wave, and you obtain from him but an insolent disdain, an unmanageable revolt; it is then you must use strength to break it, or all is lost. But why have I also said, "with tenderness"? Because, after you have broken this pride, if the child does not feel that you are inspired by the tenderest, the most devoted, a paternal, I will even say a supernatural and divine affection, he will retire broken, but he will soon rise up again and hate you; frequently both hate and despise you; then again all is lost. On this point there remain some particular remarks important to be made. Those children usually revealed themselves, and their pretended perfection burst forth in some great fault, about seventeen or eighteen years of age, sometimes even before, and it was most frequently on the following occasions: — If their habitual success suddenly failed them when they went into a higher class, if, in changing the professor, they met one less favorable to them, it was usually then that the wound of their heart (*plaga cordis*), say the Scriptures, discovered itself to their masters and themselves. Sometimes they suddenly showed a strange aversion to their new class, a profound indignation against the new professor; they avoided him, and tried not to meet him in recreation; they turned aside their looks, or regarded him from afar with eyes full of anxiety and resentment. At other times this change was owing to the awakening of a sentiment which had been dormant in their hearts, and of which they themselves were ignorant during the innocuous days of childhood, and on account of the active occupations of the young scholar. This sentiment of which I speak relates to the social condition. The appearance of fellow-scholars, whose families were of higher position, richer than theirs, gave birth to bitter comparisons and impotent desires; in the dark vexation of their rebellious pride and guilty jealousy, they felt an embarrassment with their parents, and were less happy to see them. Their temper, their language, their mien, was altered; and we know not to what should be attributed this strange and evil transformation. It was caused by the vilest of all pride having taken possession of them.

This phenomenon of perversion manifests itself sometimes from fifteen to eighteen years of age, and, as I have already said, in young people who have never had a single reproach made to them until then. Oh, what profound and skilful tenderness is necessary to win back these poor souls — to triumph over this crisis! It is the finest exercise of the gift of bringing up youth, and also the most worthy of that holy mission; every means is, then, good, when inspired by the heart and devotion. One of the mildest, and perhaps the most efficacious, that I at least have tried, is to go straight to the fact, straight to the heart of the child. I have called him to me;

said to him, tenderly, paternally, You are sad, my child; this goes badly, placing my hand on his heart; you appear to me less happy — let us see, have you not become a little less good? — that often happens without one being aware of it himself; as for me, I have no reproach to make you; but you, are you satisfied with yourself and others? Are you not hurt by somebody or something? Let us honestly seek out the guilty one; is he around you, or within yourself? Is it not pride that troubles you? In this ill-humor which you cannot define, is there not somewhat of a grudge against God, His Providence, and all the world? It seems to me that nothing around you has changed — your parents, your masters, are still the same to you. May it not be you who are a little changed to them? Put your hand on your heart; let your conscience, your reason, your religion, your good-nature, speak coolly before God, before your best friend. Let us discover. I have often seen these poor children melt into tears, look at me with confusion and emotion, cast themselves into my arms, and all was saved. We had no other explanation; there is a grief and shame in the soul which must be spared — it is sufficient to arouse them. What reflections may be made here, not only on the sad infirmities of our nature, but also on the resources which she offers when religion, coming to her aid, touches and enlightens her! There is one observation, alas! too universal, too incontestable, and with it I shall conclude this chapter. Original sin has impaired the most natural feelings, and also the noblest functions of the human heart. I have spoken of spoiled children, and of the parents who spoil them; are not these children frequently an example of the former of those alterations, and the parents an example of the latter? How many children do we see without gratitude to their parents, without affection, without respect for those from whom they received life, nourishment, every care, and alas, too assiduously, an education full of vanity and effeminacy! But, we must repeat in conclusion, if the children be frequently so guilty, are not the parents sometimes more so? Does not every subject we discoursed on in this chapter sadly demonstrate it? In order to be convinced, is it not sufficient to see the trouble a father and mother have not to spoil their children, and the struggles they must make against themselves to avoid this misfortune? Is it not sufficient to see the point where their good sense and uprightness become lost, and go wandering in a profound and grievous blindness? Again, the giddiness and thoughtlessness of young parents have a fatal influence. In a word, they should reflect in proper time on the principles to be followed in the education of their children. Nevertheless, how many alliances are contracted, how many children grow up without the duties of their education ever for a moment presenting themselves to the minds of their fathers and mothers; how many families, whose faults and imprudences point out to us every day that there are but too many parents who have not the least idea of the task to be performed! What deplorable mistakes, vicious management, and dangerous errors! How can we expect from such teachers a regular rule, a system of education based on just principles, modified according to the wants that present themselves? What can become of the child given up to himself, false in his early development, and deprived of healthy moral culture? This is what Fénelon asks himself in pointing out the dreadful consequences of this negligence and this blindness: "What," said he, "will become of children, who, in the end, make up the human species, if their mothers spoil them from their earliest years? The disorders of men are frequently caused by the bad education they receive from their mothers." What, then, should they do? They should reflect, anticipate, act firmly and persistently, whatever it may cost. They go on from day to day, till children of five or six can hardly be endured; they are amiable, they laugh at their faults and pretty tricks, they amuse themselves with their graceful sauciness, not wishing to remember that these children of five or six will soon be twenty and thirty, and that they will make their parents pay dearly for the misfortune of having spoiled them — that is to say, lost them. Montaigne says: "That a genuine and well-regulated affection should spring from and increase with our knowledge of our children, and then, if they will it, the natural inclination keeping pace with reason, cherishes them with a truly paternal friendship. How frequently is it not the contrary, and do we not usually feel ourselves more concerned with the plays and puerile follies of our children, than with their more improved actions afterwards, as if we loved them for our pastime — even as apes, not as men!"[1] What Montaigne says is bitter, but not wanting in justness. As for me, whenever I was condemned to witness the blindness and the weakness of these parents who knew only how to spoil their children, when I saw them play with these faults which become, later on, such terrible, and sometimes such cruel passions, I repeated to myself, with sorrow, the words of the Scripture: "The whelp will become a lion; he who plays with his child will some day weep." A mother once expressed this with an energy perhaps still more frightful; some one recounted to her that a young woman, in speaking of the education of her children, and the cares it brought on her, said: "It is twenty years of torture." "She deceives herself," replied this mother, who had been enlightened by a much longer experience: "it is at twenty the torture begins."

[1] Montaigne, Essays, b. ii. chap. viii.

CHAPTER IV.

THE CHILD; SOME ADVICE ON HIS EARLY EDUCATION.

I DO not wish to dwell on these sad thoughts. It is not to grieve the hearts of mothers that I write, but to aid them in the sweet, though difficult, task which Providence has imposed upon them. If there be some among them deficient in the courage, I dare not say the intelligence, to fulfil such great duties, there is a much greater number to whom religion and love have revealed the admirable art of bringing up their children in accordance with the love of God and the wishes of nature. It is of these women, truly blessed by Heaven, I would ask in this moment some practical advice, the light and authority of which I could then present with more confidence to all mothers. Let them understand — it is not a treatise on elementary education that I intend to offer them here, but only some advice; some sketches, the bearing of which their penetration and exquisite tact will know well how to seize and apply. Others, elsewhere, have already written much on this subject. I will, then, confine myself to some essential points. Education begins even with the birth of the child. All sages, all men of experience, all masters of ethics, the pagans themselves, have proclaimed it — the day the child opens his eyes on life, and makes his first cries heard, an entire series of duties relative to his education is imposed on all around him. Be not deceived; the training of this early age is the foundation, the base, of all that his later development in more advanced education, and even his application during the whole course of his life, will receive. In everything, all depends on the principles — this is a trite saying, because so true — but it is especially with respect to education that we must take care to adhere to the best principles, to lay them down forcibly from the beginning, and follow them perseveringly. Behold the terms in which the great Bossuet remarks the decisive importance of so commencing: "If one occupies himself with his children in good time, paternal influence and good precepts can then accomplish much. On the contrary, if false and fatal maxims are once permitted to enter their minds, the tyranny of habit becomes so invincible in them, that there is no remedy which can cure the evil. To prevent it becoming incurable, it must be anticipated. And, nevertheless, what comes to pass and what is done with this first age of life?" "It is given up," says Fénelon, "to indiscreet and disorderly women; though," he adds, "it is the age when the deepest impressions are made, and which, consequently, has the greatest influence on the whole future of the child." The sages of antiquity spoke in the same manner: "You are not ignorant," said Plato, "that in everything the beginning is the great affair, especially with respect to young and tender beings; it is then they may be moulded, and receive the imprint which you wish to give them.

Considering this, shall we suffer children to hear all sorts of fables invented by the first comer, and their minds to take in opinions, most of them contrary to those which we know that they will require in mature age?" (Plato, Repub., book ii., vol. ix., pp. 105, 106.) Let us, then, permit nurses to relate to children only well-chosen fables, and to use still more care in forming their minds than their bodies. It must be acknowledged, that even Christian parents are sometimes so ignorant of their duties, so blind to all concerning the early education of their children, and especially so imprudent, so inconsiderate in the choice of those to whose care they commit them in their early years, that it is, unfortunately, but too necessary to dwell on this point, and I consider it particularly useful to bring under their notice that which paganism itself formerly said on this subject. Plutarch, in a treatise on the education of children, expresses himself with still more force than Plato: "It is necessary to use every care in order to make a good choice of the nurses intrusted with their early education. In a word, if it be necessary to mould the limbs of children immediately after their birth, that they may not contract any natural defect, we cannot too soon form also their dispositions and their manners." The mind of a child is a flexible paste, which receives without resistance every form that we wish to give it — once strengthened by age, it bends with difficulty. Seals impress themselves quickly on soft wax; in the same manner the precepts we give to these still tender minds easily become imprinted, and leave deep traces there. It is for this reason the divine Plato so expressly recommends nurses never to entertain children with ridiculous tales, which fill their minds with false and absurd ideas. Again, from the same motive, we should choose with care the young servants whom we place about children to attend or be brought up with them. It is particularly necessary they should have pure morals; in the second place, that they know their own language, and speak it correctly. Corrupt servants soon communicate to children the vices of their language and their morals. The wise Quintilian also has consecrated some fine pages to this important subject. It would be too long to quote them. I have already said, the cares given to these early years are the commencement of all that his application or development will receive later on. Everything, then, requires the most serious attention. Physical education, intellectual education, moral education, and religious education — nothing should be abandoned to chance — nothing should be done or tried at random. At this age, which, as we have seen, comprises almost the first eight or ten years of life, physical education is important. Some authors of more or less weight have given with regard to it numberless advices, among which many are wise, though mixed with strange details and thoughts, which it is impossible for us to approve of. We shall confine ourselves to desiring that this first education be not too soft, for it would thus develop beyond measure that principle of effeminacy and sensuality, which, later on, resists every effort of the most serious education, and also of grace; nor too hard, as the existence and organs of the child are still so frail. "What is most important then," says Fénelon, "is, not to push on children too much; to strengthen their organs, spare their health, and form them gradually, according to the occasions which naturally present themselves. Nevertheless, from that time, intellectual education should likewise be attended to." In the child, the labor of the understanding is prodigious. It is in these early years that his mind acquires, not only the use of language and the knowledge of sensible objects, but in the language and knowledge of purely spiritual matters a multitude of extraordinary ideas. We know that this fact has excited the admiration of all clear-sighted observers, who have recognized in this secret and almost entirely spontaneous work one of the most surprising mysteries and greatest benefits of Providence. There are two systems by which children may be spoiled in their early intellectual education; the one, that of not making them do anything; the other, that of making them do too much. If this first education be wise and foreseeing, no doubt it will take advantage of the astonishing dispositions of childhood, and this wonderful opening of the mind to everything, in order to give it simple, just, clear, and precise ideas. But it will be doubtful of the mania for creating prodigies of six or eight years old, who at fifteen or twenty become children of tender parts. If it be real, and without vanity, it will apply itself constantly to forming the speech and all the language of the child to a proper purity; it may, perhaps, attach too much importance to his learning two or three foreign languages, which will be of little use later on, in the course of his public education; and, nevertheless, his confused notions of them sometimes suffice to arrest the spring of the mind in more serious studies. The fault that I point out here is not a trifling one. Doubtless, there may be great advantages in learning and speaking at an early age some foreign languages; but if this study be badly made, badly begun, badly continued, it may produce the gravest inconvenience. Fénelon, in speaking of the fancy which reigned in his time for making young children learn Italian and Spanish, went so far as to say, "that there was much more to be lost than gained in this study." Again said he: "Even when you can advance much the mind of a child without pressing it, you should fear to do so; the danger from vanity and presumption is always much greater than the fruit of those premature educations which make so much noise; into a reservoir so small and precious we should pour only the most exquisite things." It is manifest that all this requires great attention and rare discernment. I have seen children condemned to do nothing during the finest years of their youth, from fourteen to eighteen, because from six to ten they had been overpowered and worn out with work; nevertheless, on the other side, it is very necessary to take care, that, under pretext of not fatiguing them, children are not allowed to do anything, and accustomed to live in idleness and without rule. When a child comes to a certain age without applying himself to anything, it is impossible to inspire in him a desire for study or any taste for solid things; everything serious appears sad to him; everything that requires continuous attention fatigues him; the inclination to pleasure, which is so strong during youth, the example of children of the same age who are plunged in amusement — all serve to make him fear and fly the application of an orderly and laborious life. These first studies should be extremely simple — I would almost dare to say they cannot be too much so. They should consist of reading, writing, the first elements of arithmetic, and some ideas of history and geography. That is abundantly sufficient for those early years. It is important that all be well taught, well learned, well understood. Little and well — very little and very well — is the great principle. The history of the early years of the Duke of Burgundy shows us what intellectual education can and ought to do for man at this age, and what resources it finds in him to form and improve him. We know that Fénelon, to adorn the mind of his pupil, and at the same time make him perceive his faults, composed a series of Fables and Dialogues. "We see," says M. de Bausset, "by the simplicity, the precision, the clearness, of some of these fables, that they are suited to a child, whose intellect should not be wearied, and to whose mind only that which it can understand and preserve should be presented. According as the course of instruction brought the young prince to understand their bearing, these fables assumed a more elevated style — they contained some allusions to history and mythology." In developing the intellect of his pupil, Fénelon took great care not to crush him under a weight of knowledge too great for his age; and yet he knew how, skilfully, to take advantage of every means to elevate the faculties of the child, and suitably prepare them for the highest and finest amount of great literary information. This wise temperament is very rare in our days. On the one hand, we see some children burdened at an early age with a heavy erudition, on which the science of memory has exhausted the treasury of its dates and nomenclatures; or condemned to read ridiculous little moral tracts, sometimes of a despairing dryness, sometimes of insipid sentiment, and always of an odious pedantry, anything of which they are absolutely incapable of understanding or feeling. This caused a lady of great sense to say, wittily, "that the children brought up to read Peau-d'Ane, Prince Tity, and Bluëbeard, had more imagination and real sense than all those poor children brought up to read little pedantic tracts." On the other hand, even among those destined to receive the highest literary education, how many children remain without any intellectual culture until the period of primary instruction arrives!—all their faculties lie in fallow. Sometimes it takes many years to draw them out of this sad state—frequently the most assiduous cares are not sufficient to do so; and we must consider ourselves very happy if we contrive to render them capable of learning anything at fifteen or sixteen. In fine, there remains moral and religious education, for which it is the duty of a father and a mother, worthy of that name, to devote themselves to the child from the first glimmerings of his reason and understanding. They sometimes say that this education is not suited for his age, and under this pretext, which is a serious error, they neglect to give the child, at the precise time it becomes possible, that culture which is the most important, and which he is most capable of receiving. For from that time his mind is at once a soft wax, which receives the impressions given to it, and an active faculty which begins to comprehend — from that time the propensities of the heart reveal themselves; man takes his first step, and declares himself; the features of his character become delineated; the will is exercised; the conscience formed — from that time the child can acquire the first knowledge of good and evil, the first love of truth and Christian virtue. That such is the proceeding of nature has never been disputed. Why not know how to act consistently with it? Why does the labor of teachers, who understand their task, too frequently consist of combating and uprooting the gross faults contracted and nourished at this age? And how often do they succeed in it? Fénelon has given many sensible warnings respecting this point. "From this early age," he says, "however little good the nature of children may be, they can be rendered docile, patient, steady, gay, and peaceable; instead of which, if they be neglected in this early youth, they become eager and restless all their lives; their blood burns; habits become formed; the body, still tender, and the mind, which has not yet shown a propensity for anything, incline towards evil; it forms within them a species of second original sin, which is the source of a thousand disorders when they grow up." Among the admirable counsels that Fénelon addresses to those intrusted with the moral education of early age, there are two of great importance which I wish to point out here. The first relates to the awakening of sensibility at an early age in the hearts of children. "As soon as a child is capable of feeling friendship, the only question is that of directing his affection towards persons who may be useful to him. Friendship will lead him to do almost anything desired — it is assuredly a tie to draw him to good, provided it is known how to make use of it; the only thing to fear is an excess, or a bad choice in the object of his affections." Again Fénelon said, "It is necessary to try, before children shall have lost this first simplicity of the most natural emotions, to make them taste the pleasure of a cordial and reciprocal friendship. Nothing contributes so much to it as placing about them, at first, persons who never show them any harshness, falseness, meanness, or selfishness. It would be better to tolerate near them people having other faults, but exempt from these. Again, it is necessary to praise children for everything they do through friendship, provided it be not out of place or too ardent. It is also necessary that their parents show sincere friendship to them, for children often learn even from their parents not to love anything." (Fénelon, "Educ. of Daughters.") A second counsel given by Fénelon, and one which is also of great importance, is to beware of the mania and danger of imitation among children. "It is necessary," says he, "to prevent them from mimicking ridiculous people, for these mocking and dissembling manners have something low and contrary to honest sentiments in them. We may suppose that they catch them up because the warmth of their imagination, their suppleness of body, joined with their sprightliness, make it easy for them to put on all kinds of shapes to represent what strikes them as ridiculous." This tendency in children produces innumerable evils when they are intrusted to foolish people, who know not how to restrain themselves before them. How much benefit and positive influence these wise ideas, these subtle and penetrating observations, of Fénelon would have on the education of early youth, if they were well understood and meditated on! That the impressions of those early years, the habits acquired at this age, are the strongest and most lasting, is a truth which has never been disputed; but one hardly ever bethinks himself of the practical consequences to be deduced from it. Hence, laws affecting public morals cannot be too severe — laws imposing wisdom and circumspection on all those who have access to childhood, or who are bound to give it lessons and example. As soon as childhood begins to think and feel, its mind and heart need a food to nourish them, and this food, whatsoever it may be, changes itself into their substance. The ideas, the images, which present themselves to the child, gradually form the stamp of his character, and, so to speak, the foundation of his soul. While his senses and his imagination are full of what he hears and what he sees, he prepares for himself in silence the rule of his judgments and the motive of his actions; and it is this which causes the prejudices of childhood to have so incredible a strength. It is the duty of domestic education to choose with great discretion the objects which shall first strike the eye of the child, attract his attention, and on which he will exercise the sensibility of his heart — this is what domestic education ought to do, but unfortunately does not always do among us. We have been, during too long a time, trained to despise everything, to profane everything, but still to spare childhood. We know that the degree of corruption in public morals renders it very difficult to preserve even decency in private morals. Alas! how many children no longer find safety in the paternal household, where sometimes their eyes, their ears, all their senses, receive as nourishment but a subtle and deadly poison, which penetrates into those unhappy beings without their perceiving it, and destroys in their hearts even the germs of virtue — thus imparing the gifts of Nature; and frequently minds which she has qualified for great deeds, so degenerate by education, that it is with a great effort they rise again from it! It is especially when there is question of purity of morals that the education of early youth should redouble its zeal, and surround children with the most careful precautions and strictest vigilance. Fénelon wished that they should absolutely shun public theatres and all other exciting amusements, which are only suited to give children a taste for dangerous things, and, besides, never fail to make them find all innocent pleasures insipid. He branded without mercy the guilty imprudence of so many parents who thus exposed their children, with hearts still so tender, and imaginations so lively and so fickle, to the violent shocks of theatrical amusements, to the languishing tones of that effeminate music, which serves but to enervate the powers of the mind, and render the morals of the child loose and voluptuous, and which gives so much pleasure only because the soul delivers itself up to the allurements of the senses, almost to intoxication. Fénelon went so far as to wish that children should be inspired with horror — it is the expression he uses — "horror of those poisoned amusements and other corrupting vanities, nakedness of the bosom, and every other immodesty," which people so frequently indulge in before children, or permit to them. "Nothing," said he, "can justify in these parents, before God or man, a conduct so rash, so scandalous, and so contagious for their children." Since we cannot, in the state of our morals, let childhood grow up in ignorance of vice, it would be desirable that we could make a compact with its newly-born faculties to suspend their progress, and retain them in idleness as long as possible, that they might be developed without danger. For minds entirely blank, not trained, and void of everything, would be far less removed from wisdom than those who have gathered it and carry with it perfidious seeds. Then, at least, the time of the second education would not be almost entirely wasted in combating with and destroying the vicious impressions made by the first; and a man should not be reduced to applauding himself as completely successful, when he has only succeeded in curing the evil already done. At the same time, it must be said, and I have witnessed it, that this first education is often very well commenced and admirably conducted in Christian families among us. God has given to man, from the beginning, a natural teacher, whom no one can replace. How many times has not a good mother, a pious mother, found, in her own heart and in the inspirations of piety, secrets of education a thousand times more efficacious than any pedagogic theories! I shall afford myself the consolation of speaking of them in detail when I come to treat of the rights and duties of maternal authority. At present I shall confine myself to saying, that the cares of a mother are necessary to a child, not only for the first two or three years of his life, but far beyond it. Above all, I could never approve of giving up to public education children of four or five years, to whom nothing can replace maternal care.[1] It is for the mother to arouse in her child the first glimmerings of intelligence, and the first love of good; to place upon his lips the first words of faith and virtue; to turn his first looks towards heaven; in a word, it is for the mother to endow him with a Christian soul, as she has given to him a human body; and if there be nothing so hideous as the example, happily very rare, of a mother breathing irreligion into the heart of her son, so also nothing is more moving and beautiful to see than the spectacle of a Christian mother giving to a child,

[1] It can be easily understood that I do not here condemn the Salles d'Asile, nor even the Crèche.

blessed by God, his first instruction in faith, recounting to him the touching histories of religion, teaching him to join his little hands in prayer, and making him lisp with his infantine mouth the most sacred Name. Such ought to be the first education — I more willingly call it maternal education. It should be carried on at the domestic hearth, provided the paternal household be always for this child, beginning life, a school of purity, justice, goodness, virtue, wisdom, and mildness — that nothing comes there to spoil his heart or his mind during those happy times, when thought, reason, speech, and conscience are being primitively formed in him; when the first elements of his whole intellectual and moral life are being prepared. In concluding this chapter, I would wish to pledge my readers to study Fénelon's Treatise on the Education of Daughters, because it is an incomparable book. I wished to give some extracts from it, and then I perceived I should quote the entire work. Fénelon makes in it not only the education of children, but especially that of tutors, governesses, and mothers. Pastors and catechists, themselves, will find there the most important, elevated, and fruitful instructions, particularly in chapters vi., vii., and viii., on the use of history to indoctrinate into the mind of the child the first principles of religion.

CHAPTER V.

THE RESPECT DUE TO THE DIGNITY OF CHILDHOOD IS A RELIGIOUS RESPECT.

If the child appear, in the eyes of the philosopher, enlightened by faith, a being worthy of a religious respect, it is because, besides the graces and natural prerogatives of his age, he finds something higher and more divine which should inspire this respect, and elevate him almost to God Himself. God is actually the Creator, the Father, the Model, of this child. All those artless graces on which we rest our eyes with so much complaisance are the reflections of the Divine Grace itself; and if his education should ascend so high, and be made with so religious a care, it is because, sublime creature, he bears, in the foundation of his nature, in the elevation, power, and harmony of his faculties, the likeness of God. This humble child is destined to a double kingdom. If he carries his crown worthily on earth, the kingdom of Heaven will one day be opened to him; and if we sometimes give him the name of angel, though abased beneath them here on earth, it is because God has lavished on him, as on the angels, life, intelligence, and love, and with this celestial nature all the faculties, all the gifts, all the wonderful attributes, which flow from it.

"Let us make man to our image and our likeness:" these admirable words, says Bossuet, "reveal to us, that, in creating man, God proposed no other model but Himself," and that He wished to make the features of His perfection and His glory shine forth magnificently in the human creature. I do not wish to dilate further than is suitable on this mysterious subject; at the same time, I cannot but remark what a surprising trinity is to be met with in the unity of a created and imperfect nature, and how lively an image and surprising a likeness of the most high God we catch a glimpse of in it. God is life, intelligence, unbounded love. God is truth, beauty, supreme goodness. Well, it has pleased this God that these constitutive perfections of His own essence should be the foundation even of being in this weak child. God has wished that the highest powers of His divine nature should be reflected in the dawning faculties of this being so lowly. This child, then, lives, thinks, loves, as God lives, thinks, and loves. The true, the beautiful, the good, should be the essential and only object of intellectual and moral instruction in his education. And it is in the perfect accord of the great human faculties with the true, the beautiful, and the good, with the truth, beauty, and supreme goodness, that the principle of harmony, repose, plenitude, and power of these faculties will be found. Such is the work of education. This sublime theory of the faculties of man, which at present I confine myself to indicating, and which further on I will explain, is but the principle and foundation of the theory of education itself. This theory rules the development and exercise of the human faculties; it reveals the play, nature, and action of them in the grown man as in the child; and, at the same time, it is it alone which enlightens the science, languages, literatures, poetry, and arts which are taught to him. In all these faculties God at first entirely appears; His name, His splendor, burst forth from all sides, and cause to glitter like the light of a divine day all the beauties of human nature, and all the riches with which God has endowed it. The Divine perfection, to the image of which this child was created, is then the end, the model, the image, the essential type, of the education which he should receive. "Let us make man to our image and likeness:" the word of God could not be more decisive. It is thus that God becomes for this child at once the perfection of his being, the immortal nourishment of his intellect, the inspiration of his love, and the entire life of his soul. This should explain why I have said that education was a divine work, and that the respect due to the nature and dignity of this child was a religious respect, and should elevate him almost to God. But what it is also necessary to understand here, is, that this fine and great nature, that all these gifts of the Creator, require germination and growth, and of themselves solicit development and the culture of this religious respect. Life, intelligence, and love, wit, talent, genius, good sense, good taste, will, character, conscience, letters, sciences, arts, even industry, religion, morality, truth, virtue, — all these great and divine gifts of humanity are without light and without name in a child, and will remain buried in the depths of his nature, if care be not taken to study them with respect, and cultivate them religiously. There is the beautiful work of education; but once more, a respectful education only can satisfy such noble claims, and correspond to their sublime instincts. A devotion, a respect, truly, sincerely religious, alone can suitably cultivate the wonderful gifts of the Creator, elevate these fine faculties to the strength of their natural integrity and establish them in the power and plenitude of their action, adorn them with their finest growth, and at length crown them with the flowers and fruits of science and virtue. And behold why education, such as I conceive it ought to be, is but the most profound evidence of the respect of which human nature is worthy. High as this theory may appear, it is the foundation on which the edifice of the entire education rests and should be raised. Ah! without doubt, this work is not easy; it has vast proportions, and, in its apparent simplicity, offers numerous and imposing aspects; and every time that one does not apply himself to comprehend, undertake, and do it in all its magnitude, he is wanting in respect for it. Yes, every time that one does not devote himself to cultivate religiously, and elevate nature and human dignity in the child; every time that he neglects to form in him man such as God has conceived him, man such as God has created him, man such as God wishes he should be formed and completed; every time that he does not this, he betrays, he violates, the respect which is due to this child and his original greatness; and, I ought to add, such misfortune is not rare. Teachers of youth should never forget that the child is man himself, the depositary of all the gifts of God, all the hopes of humanity; and, young though he be, he is already invested with all the grace, all the dignity, which God has communicated to human nature. The remembrance of this will suffice to sustain the courage of teachers, and prevent them from failing in the noble and laborious task to which they have devoted themselves. Certainly, when the Creator wished to make man, He did not labor negligently or disdainfully at this great work; it was not a play for Him, as the creation of the material world had been. It is worthy of remark that God no longer makes use of this brief and imperious word, with which he caused to come out of the eternally sterile bowels of nothing the multitude of common creatures which charm our eyes, including amongst them light and the sun. No; He meditated within Himself, pronounced a word of advice, and, if I may say it, of respect — this great and immortal word, "Let us make man to our image and likeness." He then acted with the gravity worthy of so solemn a work. The creation of man was, above all, the result of a supreme deliberation, an action entirely divine, and, in fine, a breath, an inspiration of eternal life, *spiraculum vitæ.* Such was the greatness of the creation of man; such ought to be the work, the gravity, the greatness, of his education; such the respect which is due to him. Behold what is the chief point to be well understood when one takes up this labor. I shall now enter into some practical details. The end of education is to form man; but what does this mean, and what is the real task of the teacher? Here it is. Man has, at the same time, body and soul, understanding, will, heart, and conscience: God has made him so.

To form man is, then, to make the child attain all the development, all the elevation, all the strength, all the beauty, of which his physical and intellectual, moral and religious, faculties are susceptible. It is to give to his body the vigor, the pliancy, the agility, necessary for the good service of the soul; but that, be it understood, is still but a trifle. The pagans themselves found that man is a noble spectacle only when the beauty and strength of the soul are in harmony with the beauty and strength of the body.[1] *Gratior et pulchro veniens in corpore virtus* (Virgile). *Mens sana in corpore sano* (Juvenal).

Again, to form man is especially to give to his mind all the fine knowledge, reveal to him all the noble doctrine, which will be the ornament and light of his life; it is to make him acquire all his strength and all his capacity by suitable exercises and intellectual labor; it is to develop in him judgment, reasoning, taste, penetration, memory, imagination, facility of elocution; in a word, thought and speech, those two great prerogatives of humanity. To form man, as God requires him, is at the same time to strengthen his character, confirm his will, enlighten his conscience, and inspire in his heart a generous sensibility. It is to place and nourish in his soul every virtuous inclination which will induce him to fulfil the law of duty towards his Creator, towards

[1] Plato. Repub. book iii. chap. ix.

himself, society, and all his kind. Without doubt, all this is a great deal, but it is not yet all; if we stopped there, the work would be imperfect, or rather it would be little short of utter ruin. We have already seen that man has numerous deplorable faults; he is fortunate when they are but defects of his good dispositions. In a good education these dispositions are strengthened by the defects themselves, which they absorb, and over which they gradually triumph; thus in the end, and thanks to the struggle, becoming virtues. On the contrary, in a bad education these defects carry away and crush the good dispositions, and become vices. What, then, is the great, and frequently the most painful, labor of the teacher? It is this. If he wish, as he ought to wish, to establish the child in the legitimate and entire possession of the faculties of his nature, if he wish to make him a man by that means, and a man worthy of the name, he will not confine himself to increasing in the heart of this child every inclination to duty, and developing his good dispositions; he will diligently apply himself to study his defects, root out his dangerous tendencies, reform his bad habits, and correct his vices, if unfortunately they are already to be found in this young creature; he will anticipate, if he can, the awakening of the passions, or at least control them strongly and wisely at the proper time. It is at this price only the work can be accomplished; and for this reason I have said that education is essentially a work of respect. I do not know anything which requires more respectful devotedness than this painful labor. Without the thought of God, without a religious respect for human nature, one could never sincerely and courageously labor to correct, reform, and elevate it. I recapitulate all this: education ought to mould man, make of the child a man, that is to say, give him a strong and healthy body, a trained and penetrating mind, an upright and sound reason, a fertile imagination, a sensible and pure heart, and all that, in the highest degree, of which the child is susceptible. Such is its work; such are its benefits; such the high and vast idea which ought to preside over every step of human education, maternal education, primary education, secondary education. Education never leaves man till it institutes him in life, and institutes him as man complete. It is then, from this high point of view, conformably with that beautiful Latin expression which Quintilian and Bossuet make use of, that education may be called the *institution* of man. It is then is accomplished the work of religious respect due to the noble creature of God. But, they will say to me, is it always necessary to elevate it so high? May we not do less? Where, then, are the teachers worthy of the name? I am not charged with resolving this last question; but I answer without hesitation, No; we may not do less. Education, under pain of being incomplete, of leaving man unfinished, and, consequently, profoundly wanting in the dignity of this beautiful nature, should make of the child a man in all his integrity. It should put him fully in possession of himself; it should, consequently, develop, polish, elevate, all his noble faculties as completely as it is possible to do it; it cannot neglect any of them. Otherwise it is an imperfect work; it is a bad education; it is a miserable work; and when it is considered that this work is man himself, of whom God has said, "Let us make him to our image and likeness," one is tempted to ask those unworthy teachers by what right they bring a rash hand over the work and the image of God, to disfigure it; over such beautiful and such pure hopes, to wither them; over such high faculties, to ruin them. We are justly surprised at this guilty negligence, this haughty disdain, from which education so frequently suffers. In fine, we are deeply irritated with this sacrilegious contempt, and, I will say, all these mercenary, hypocritical cares, of which childhood is so frequently the object and the victim. I like to think that this evil arises more usually from want of intelligence and reflection; they do not know, and, let us acknowledge, they do not attach sufficient importance to knowing, what this great work of education is. It is true, they do not dispute the radical necessity of it for all, nor the immense influence it has on the individual, on the family, on all society; they do not even refuse to recognize that its end is to mould, to elevate, and make man perfect; but that of which they are ignorant, or know but partly, is, that to attain this end, the essential, proper character of education, is to cultivate religiously, develop and strengthen, all the faculties of man, without any unworthy exception. They do not understand that human education ought to be like man himself, whom it seeks to form, simple, uniform, constant, complete. Man actually has received nothing from God that education can neglect; he is a being worthy of elevation on every account. The integrity of his education is the providential law of his life and his future. It cannot be knowingly or negligently frustrated without betraying him in the most guilty manner; and, nevertheless, they hardly ever inquire for the instruments or the means which education can and ought to make use of to exercise its great action and accomplish its entire work with respect. Hence so many deplorable educations, which are, at the same time, the misfortune of the pupils and the shame of the teachers.

CHAPTER VI.

OF HUMAN NATURE IN THE CHILD; ON HIS DEFECTS; NECESSITY OF KNOWING THEM WELL, AND CORRECTING THEM IN HIM.

I.

IT is necessary to return to the child, and cast a supreme and profound look into his soul, and even into the greatest recesses and inmost depths of his nature; for it is there that the work of education is really to be done; it is there that the obstacles as well as the resources lie: it is there that every effort should be brought to bear. *Hoc opus, hic labor est.* But it should be well understood that a soul, the nature of a child, is quite a world; we may say, in the words of the Holy Scriptures, it is an abyss (*Abyssum es cor* — Ecclus. xlii. 18) which can never sufficiently be explored and enlightened. And the Scriptures add of this heart of man, that it is at once inscrutable and bad, *Cor pravum et inscrutabile.* (Jerem. xvii. 9.) Inscrutable as the heights of heaven and the depths of earth, *Sicut cœlum sursum et terra deorsum.* (Prov. xxv. 3.) And, nevertheless, if one has not scrutinized this abyss, if one has not fathomed this heart in every way, he is unsuited to the great work of education; for, once again, it is not on the surface, but in the interior of the soul, that this work is to be done. It must be an every-day labor and study; and, willingly applying to this knowledge of children the words of St. Paul, I will say to masters, *Hæc meditare in his esto, insta in illis.* The heart of the child is the book which must be pondered on and searched into unceasingly; it is a never-ending study; there will always be something to discover in it, and you will be suited to your work only in proportion as you become clever in reading this living book and fathoming all its secrets. The interior radical obstacle springs up again unceasingly; it is the foundation even of human nature which is spoiled; these are the defects and vices, the fatal germs of which are in us, as a consequence of original perversion. Plato has said, "The new-born child is not good; but he may become so if he be well brought up." Certainly not; the new-born child is not good. The evil germs are within, and wait but age to blow. It is with these evil germs, and sometimes with the most vicious inclinations, in a word, it is with the profound defects of this nature, that the struggle must be carried on, but with the aid of means for education far superior to all those that Plato ever knew. It has been said that the human soul is, in the child, a blank tablet, where nothing has yet been written: it may be so, though there is much to be said thereon; but at least it has certainly already its *virtualities*, all its powers; and if it be fertile for good, unfortunately it has also an undoubted fecundity for evil. The maladies from which the human soul suffers, and consequently the education of the child, are as innumerable as those from which physical life and health suffer: education, the physician of the soul, whose mission is the cure of these ills, should, like the physician of the body, begin by studying them well, so as to know them well. In this soul there is not only evil, but there is good; there are not only defects, but there are good dispositions; education, at the same time that it corrects the faults and cures the evil, should also develop and elevate the good dispositions, and, as St. Paul says, "conquer the evil through the good." For this there must be not only great zeal, but great discernment, and the emmployent of serious remedies, without which the ills of humanity can never be cured.

II.

In one of those admirable parables, of a divine simplicity, by which our Lord formerly instructed his disciples, the parable of the cockle and the good grain, there is a striking image of that which is the great rock of education, and also the great duty of the teacher. Without doubt, this parable may be applied in all its details, and, above all, to the mixture of the good and the wicked on earth; but we may likewise, in some manner, usefully and truly apply it to the mixture of good and evil dispositions which are to be found in children and every human creature. God—and this is especially true with respect to children brought up in a house of Christian education—God has abundantly sown in these children the good grain; at first, through the good inclinations which he has given them at their birth, then by Baptism and the other sacraments, and by all the early graces of a good education. There is no nature, however sterile or disagreeable it may appear, which has not its rich depths of valuable qualities, which education should cultivate and develop; but there is likewise in the nature of every child, not excepting the most amiable, side by side with the good qualities, all that multiplying family of numerous faults, all those vicious germs, of which we have spoken, and which are, according to the evangelical parable, the cockle among the good grain: the enemy has come during a fatal night, and in the midst of the good seed has cast the bad, and withdrawn himself: *super seminavit zizania, et abiit.* Then, when the seed grows, the cockle suddenly appears in the midst of the good plants, showing itself like a dead, drooping grass, like noxious weeds.

What happens then? The servants of the father of the family are quite surprised: they ought not to be so; for, since the original fall, this mixture is natural, inevitable, and should be expected; but persons are deceived so easily! indignation soon succeeds surprise: they wish — and on the moment, as the Gospel says — to tear up this fruit of malediction: *vis colligimus ea?* That is to say — no longer to use a figure of speech otherwise so clear — parents, or the directors of a house of Christian education, after having been ministers and witnesses of the most abundant favors from God, recognize with terror, that, parallel with their work, another work has been done — and that, in souls where grace had been profusely shed, unexpected faults and vices have silently sprung up, which compromise all their labor. Alas! they do not easily consent to acknowledge that it is sometimes during their sleep that the evil has been done, and that they have not always, perhaps, been sufficiently watchful: *Dum dormirent homines!* Then one of two things comes to pass: either they delude themselves as to the evil which they feel they have not the courage to strive against — each takes his part, and again enters into his sleep; or they become transported, and would wish without delay to ravage the whole field, in order to tear up with one stroke all this cockle, that it may no longer trouble them, and that they may take their repose again. But, in the culture of souls, it does not suit to act thus; this headstrong zeal is not true zeal. Like the servants in the Gospel, they must have recourse to the wisdom of the Master of the harvest, and recollect the answer given by the father of the family to the laborers, who knew not how to repair the evil caused by their sleep but by the fire of a passing and destructive zeal: *Vis imus et colligimus ea?* said they. No, he replied to them: *Ne forte colligentes zizania, eradicetis simul cum eis et triticum.* This answer is profoundly divine. Assuredly, there is no question of allowing to subsist in souls the faults which spring up in them. The necessity of extirpating the bad seed is manifestly to be deduced from these terrible words of the father of the family: "At the time of the harvest I will say to the reapers, Gather first the bad grass, and tie it in sheaves, to cast it into the fire." The salvation of the souls in which this impure germs displays itself manifestly depends on the extirpation of their defects; but great prudence and most careful precaution must be used, in order not to tear up the wheat at the same time with the cockle. If the evil germs be not destroyed in good time, when the last harvest arrives all will be lost. But in this first harvest of souls, cultivated by education, great care is necessary not to extirpate the good dispositions with the bad; they sometimes touch so closely; and, if one be not very attentive, there is great danger of taking one for the other; for this work of discernment and enlightened extirpation, it is necessary to study well the depths of human nature, that is to say, to know the defects that shoot from the bottom of the heart, and may stifle there the grace planted by God: it is necessary to know them, and, at the same time, to know their remedies. It is also necessary to study well the good inclinations of nature, and that which may be drawn from them. In a word, it is necessary to recognize the distinct nature of good and evil; of the good and evil germs, their different roots, their numerous ramifications. And this is what impetuous zeal, false zeal, can rarely decide. This zeal is almost always as indolent as passionate. It knows only how to repose in a deplorable sleep, or to wake up abruptly, tear up all, overturn all, and destroy everything in a soul. True zeal has another spirit, another mode of action. It is to it that the instructions we are about to read are addressed.

CHAPTER VII.

TWO IMPORTANT OBSERVATIONS ON THE SAME SUBJECT.

I.

YOUTH is the proper time for the correction of faults. Whatever evil germs may be hidden in the soul of the child, thanks to God, they never render his education impossible. It is written that God has made man curable: *sanabiles fecit.* Education — a Christian education — is singularly powerful, and frequently works miracles; it is the glory, nay, the triumph, of education, to struggle with a difficult nature, conquer, correct, and transform it. But the chief point in this work is to begin in good time; otherwise it is soon compromised, not to say impossible. In childhood and youth the faults have not yet struck deep roots, nor acquired rapid growth. All is still tender and weak. Later on, habit will become — and habit soon becomes — second nature, the resistances of which are terrible. The story of the solitary of the Thebaid and his palm-tree is known; but it may be useful to bring it again under the notice of parents and masters: — Wishing to make a young man understand the importance of beginning in good time to correct his faults, he showed him a vigorous palm-tree, which, during many years, spread its shade around; he ordered him to tear up this old inhabitant of the desert; but when, after unheard-of exertions, the young man could not even succeed in loosening it, the solitary pointed out to him another tree, newly planted, and told him to try his strength against it. A few efforts sufficed to throw the young palm-tree on the ground. It is thus that, in youth, faults easily yield to the pressure of good will; whilst, later on, strengthened, hardened by age, they become like another nature, and frequently can only be rooted out with terrible difficulty: for this reason, a man, venerable by his experience, his wisdom, and his virtues, as well as his great age, said, in speaking of the education of the Petits Seminaires, that it nearly always decided everything, whether good or evil, for the entire life. This is true. I have already discoursed at great length on this particular point. I will add but a single word. The correction of the faults of children should not be reserved till the period of their public education: it is in the family itself, and as soon as they begin to display themselves, they should be recognized, combated, and extirpated, if such can be done. It is true, there are some faults which appear later on, when certain circumstances provoke their appearance; but nearly all manifest themselves during the tenderest years, in the spontaneity of this first blossoming of childhood. Well, it is then our eyes should be open and always watchful to everything which indicates, everything which reveals, a hidden fault. Are parents usually solicitous to do this? So far from seeking to discover the faults of their children, will parents consent even to recognize them when pointed out to them? Oh! they are extremely clear-sighted with respect to all the amiabilities of these dear children; they know very well how to see in them what they have, and even what they have not; but as to faults, it is another thing; they are blind to them: paternal and maternal tenderness places a veil over their eyes. This blindness, more or less voluntary on the part of parents, is one of the greatest miseries of early education; and their weakness in correcting these faults when at length they burst forth, their impotence in arming themselves with a salutary rigor to set right these natures, more or less spoiled by flattery or effeminate complaisance, are not less fatal. Is not this what too frequently occurs in the effeminacy and enervation of the morals of our time? The ancient severity of the fathers and mothers of families is very rare to-day: they begin by adulating the child, looking on him as a little perfection; then, when this pretended perfection at last appears what it is, absolutely insupportable, they free themselves of it. After having treated the child as a graceful idol, and being amused with him during his first years, when the burden of paternity is less heavy, or the enjoyment of it more lively, when the burden weighs upon them, when the caprices of the idol are a little less easy to satisfy, they send the idol to school. They reserve to themselves seeing him again on certain appointed days, amusing him, being amused by him, but so as not to keep him too long, and to place, before difficulties shall have had time to arise again, the grates of the college between him and them."[1]

Certainly, by this time the evil is already great, and the education of the child much compromised; at the same time, nothing is yet to be despaired of. A child at ten or twelve years of age may have deplorable habits, but they are not inveterate. The life of a good house of education may suddenly break them off, and, as it were, open a new era; rule, study, piety, may happily take the place of whim, caprice, of indolent labor; but it is time, without further delay, to seize the child vigorously, and take up energetically, and from the ground-work, the education so deplorably commenced. I repeat it, the great duty of the teacher, his noblest and most laborious mission, is to be met with here — *Hoc opus, hic labor est.*

II.

It is not sufficient to know the defects of children well; it is necessary to make them know them.

Thus, then, it is a work of profound correction and extirpation that there is question of doing; delicate, courageous, persevering, and indispensable work. Without this work, we might give a varnish of politeness to the surface, and gild the outside; but

[1] M. de Champagny, from whom I borrow these penetrating remarks, adds: "They expend at the feet of this little tyrant, in his early years, all the solicitude, all the cares, all the caresses, all the funds of tenderness, with which they are provided. But the funds become exhausted, tenderness becomes wearied, indolence supervenes; at the period when serious education ought to begin, they

that would be doing nothing: the work within, the work to the heart — to the root — is the necessary work.

It is there, in accordance with the forcible language of the Holy Books, that it is necessary to root out and to plant, to destroy and to build. Yes; to the teacher of youth, to him also, it is said, as to the prophet, *Ego posui te ut evellas et destruas, ut ædifices et plantes.* Every teacher of youth who does not understand it thus, understands nothing of his real mission. Virgil, in his graceful language, formerly said to the cultivator of new vineyards, "When the season of spring arrives, and when the promised fruit covers the tree with abundant flowers and bends down its odorous branches, oh! then, then observe it!" — *Contemplator item, cum se nux plurima sylvis. Induet in florem, et ramos curvabit olentes.* For all these flowers will not one day give fruit; some of them are false hopes, which will deceive the cultivator. I will say the same to the cultivator of youth: this age is properly the season of spring; everything opens and blossoms in those young plants, in those young souls; but look well into them; *contemplator* — consider attentively what there is in the heart, in the calix of these flowers, and see if they promise good or bad fruits. Look into them closely, and that, at the same time, for your own instruction, so that, being better enlight-

have no longer heart for the work; the child, too much fawned upon, becomes ungovernable; they hasten to remit to the cares of public teachers the undertaking of his education, commenced with so much love, but so badly commenced!" — *On Home Education.*

ened, your influence may have a more serious effect, and also, when you shall have discovered the truth, for the instruction of the child, in order that he may unite his action with yours against himself. For it ought not to be forgotten, in order to correct defects, the master alone can do nothing: the child cannot remain passive in such a work: he should co-operate in it by a free concurrence; but, to do that, he must be enlightened with respect to himself. To labor for the correction of his defects, he must first know them, and know them through the master; of himself, and by himself alone, he could not acquire this knowledge. Frequently men cannot do it; how could a child do it? We are aware the knowledge of our defects is as difficult as it is necessary; hence nothing is more uncommon. He knows his faults easily; and, no doubt, that is something; but he does not know that which, nevertheless, may be much more necessary — the defects which are the origin of them. He knows the names of the gross vices in general, and sometimes he even casts a rapid glance on himself to see if he be defiled with them; but because the defects, of early youth especially, have not yet arrived at the degree of malignity which makes them vices, he finds himself pure from these great stains, and considers himself in safety. And, nevertheless, the defects most to be feared grow then, and become strong in the privacy of the soul.

In a house of Christian education, for example, it is difficult for young people not to know their faults. In the prescribed duties of each day, a thousand circumstances recall them to mind, and, consequently, transgressions are too evident not to be perceived; they are facts on which it is impossible for them to shut their eyes. They acknowledge their faults then, and make resolutions on the subject; but these resolutions are seldom efficacious, because they do not strike at the source of the faults they commit; because they do not really know their defects; they do not wish to acknowledge their real defects; they seldom examine themselves on their hidden defects; and, I add, nothing is more difficult to find than one who can aid us to know ourselves — one who will make us know our defects. It is easy enough to find a friend who consents to warn us of our faults; but it is very difficult to find one who consents to enlighten us on our defects. Warning a person of his faults is a different matter from enlightening him on his defects. The one is simple, even easy, enough; the other requires not only great zeal, but discernment of mind and a courageous sincerity. Among men, friendship and truth may here be of great assistance; and, nevertheless, how rarely one loves a friend truly enough to enlighten him on his defects! But among young people, among children, especially, what can these friendly admonitions be, save and except warnings on their faults rather than on their defects? and that can be imagined. Young people want the experience and the qualities requisite for discerning defects; and frequently, even when they do perceive them, they have neither the necessary authority to make them known, whether they wish or not, to those of their school-fellows who have not thought of asking such a service of them, nor the courage to declare them even to those who interrogate them on the subject. Who, then, can render this important service to young people save those whose office makes it a duty — directors, professors, masters, and parents also? Children are perfectly sensible of this, as the words, full of good sense and simplicity, which one of them wrote to his superior, prove, saying, "You only can be my great monitor." But I should add here, in speaking of the defects of children, I think of others as well as children; and while recommending masters to study their pupils attentively, that they may know them well and assist them to correct themselves, I recommend them to do first, on their own account, and for themselves, the same work. I take this grave admonition to myself also. No one can speak of the defects of human nature, without being, as the Church somewhere says, *memor conditionis suæ*, without thinking of himself and his weaknesses. No one here on earth is actually in better condition than his brethren; no one has a right to cast the first stone at his neighbor; and when it is one's duty to give such grave instructions, and, if I may so express myself, lecture others, he must, above all, be well prepared himself. After all, each of us is chiefly interested here; each has seriously much to do for himself. St. Augustine said, "There is no fault committed by a man of which another man may not be capable, if the grace of God do not preserve him from it." We are all kneaded with the same leaven; we all partake, as St. Paul formerly said, of the same mass of original corruption; and, as each is the workman more immediately charged with the care of his own salvation, with knowing himself well, knowing well his own defects, and laboring to correct them, it is incontestably here that each should begin. Moreover, knowledge of one's self is the best means of knowing others; and from every point of view, the greatest service which a teacher can receive, is, beyond dispute, that of being enlightened by a true, sincere friend on his personal defects. Who does not know one of the wisest maxims proclaimed by antiquity—*Nosce te ipsum;* and St. Augustine's most frequent prayer to our Lord was, *Noverim te, noverim me!*

One year, when I was Superior of the Petit Seminaire of Paris, during six weeks I spoke for half an hour every evening, to all the masters and pupils, on this important subject. Not only had they the courage to listen to the harsh, painful matters I had to speak of; but, without my knowledge, they took notes, and that in short-hand, of what I then said, and these form the foundation of the present work. Be that as it may. At the Petit Seminaire of Paris, I did not consider the house in good working order until I had directed the efforts of all to the study and correction of defects, until I had inspired the children with the real desire of knowing all their defects, and the masters with the zeal to admonish and enlighten them; and, the better to fulfil this duty, to admonish and enlighten themselves first.

CHAPTER VIII.

OF THE DIFFERENT SPECIES OF DEFECTS.

THE question then is, for all and each to know his own defects, and even those of others, if it be his mission to correct them; the question is that of discerning them in the faults which manifest them, in the secret recesses of the heart which conceals them, and by the side of the excellent qualities with which they are to be found mixed, and of which they are sometimes but the excess or the abuse. All this study, all this discernment, is difficult. Yes, difficult: for, firstly, there are some defects which we do not know; secondly, there are some we do not wish to know; thirdly, there are some we know, but which we do not wish to correct. There are some defects which we do not know; nothing is more dangerous; they germinate, become rooted, and silently take possession of the soul; and, when they have borne the bitterest fruits, it is generally too late to uproot them; at least it becomes very difficult. The soul is then like an old, rugged, knotty trunk, that has cast deep, interwoven, living roots into the earth; this trunk opposes to the arm which wishes to move it an obstinate resistance; and if, after great toil, we succeed in uprooting it, the soil where it had buried its roots is completely upturned. I am about to give an example, very common in houses of education, of those hidden, unperceived defects, which, for want of knowing them, are imprudently allowed to increase. Here is a child, sensible, docile, laborious, intelligent, full of ardor and emulation: he has good marks, good places — has always given satisfaction. But gradually, with the pleasure of success and praise, legitimate, without doubt, but little watched over, self-love, vanity, and pride glide into the heart of the child, spread themselves, and insensibly increase in it. Nevertheless, while all goes on well, no one perceives anything; but a check arrives, or a cloud comes over his conduct; the child deserves a bad place, or receives a bad mark; suddenly vexation displays itself, vanity is wounded, pride becomes irritated, and a sudden, unexpected burst reveals in this child, believed to be so good and docile, a terrible defect which was never suspected, but which was there, growing every day, already old and deep-rooted, and which, unknowingly, was nourished as a pleasure. Thus one may have in him envy, temper, sensuality, anger, and many other defects; because we are ignorant of them, we believe him exempt from them; because they have not yet burst forth, we think they do not exist, and we do not labor to cure them. What do I say? as in this child, perhaps we cherish them, and, by deplorable imprudence, feed the fire which smoulders under the ashes. And the misfortune is so much the greater, because time alone is powerless to enlighten him; on the contrary, the longer this ignorance lasts, the more profound it usually becomes. Thus we pass long years with defects that every one perceives, every one suffers from; which have on a thousand occasions produced fruits of bitterness, and their existence was not even suspected. In this manner we find people arrive at the age of forty, fifty years, and beyond it, without ever having the least suspicion of a defect which has been the misfortune of their lives. At length, some day, a courageous friend, taking advantage of a favorable opportunity, dares to call their attention to the evil: — "You believe that?" they say to him quite surprised. "Yes, examine yourself from this point of view, and you will see that there is there what explains such imprudence, such misfortune, perhaps all your vexations, all your faults." What then? either they recognize their defects, and a superhuman courage is necessary for the enterprise of correcting them and keeping them from falling into despair, or they close their eyes to them, and persevere in their blindness, which renders the misfortune irreparable. Secondly, there are, then, some defects which we do not know; but, what is still worse, there are some *we do not wish to know.* The degree to which this extends, even among children, is really extraordinary. For example, there are children naturally false, dissembling, insincere, without frankness, untruthful; untruthful from taste, from vice of nature; will they acknowledge this shameful defect to themselves? No, they are deficient in sincerity with respect to themselves as well as to others; they will lie to themselves as they lie to everybody. The truth is, that, if they do not see their defects the greater part of the time, it is also true, and still more grievous to add, they hardly ever wish to see them. There is in the bottom of the heart a secret tendency to self-love which makes them not wish to know themselves, in order not to have to condemn themselves; or, again, sometimes it is a secret indolence which does not permit them to try and make the necessary efforts to correct themselves. Here are the two unacknowledged sources of this voluntary ignorance, self-love and indolence. *Noluit intelligere ut bene ageret*, says the Scripture. Or rather, if they consent to cast their eyes on their exterior defects, they never consent to open them to their interior defects, to the defects in the depth of their nature, because that touches too closely on *self*, that is to say, on what they hold nearest and dearest in the world. On all this they take the part of flattering themselves, and defend themselves against others to the utmost. They will not endure anything touching what they call *conscience, character;* the slightest contradiction on this point irritates; the least observation wounds; every reprimand exasperates. It is curious, but profoundly sad, to see these poor people, watchful, on their guard, and, as may be said, armed from head to foot against whosoever wishes to attempt making them become a little better informed. Again, they consent to be warned of a fault; that is an exterior, striking fact; it comes under notice, it may well be agreed to; besides, it may be accidental, and does not imply a vice of nature; but as to a defect, it is another thing; that is in us, it is ourselves, they feel the whole bearing of the warning in this place, and it immediately protests, by a kind of instinctive instantaneous repulsion; for this reason, in admonishing, to pass from a fault to a defect is always a delicate affair, which is endured with difficulty. The above is a very common, but very dangerous disposition, even among children; it is only a father, a mother, a clear-sighted superior, a watchful and zealous director, a professor heartily devoted to his pupils, who can prudently, usefully, efficaciously, admonish them; but the essential condition of success is, that these admonitions be given with great friendship and kindness; they will only be received with docility if the child be convinced of the affection of him who gives them, and he must always feel it, even in the heat of words. Thirdly, in fine, there are defects which they know, but do not wish to correct; and in this case there is positive infidelity to duty and virtue — an infidelity as guilty as fatal; and alas! it is necessary to add, that this very frequently occurs. From all we have already gone through on this subject, we must then conclude that it is of the highest importance to know one's defects, and as soon as possible; that it is necessary to wish to know them, and consequently the means of seeking them out; in fine, that one can never be excused for not wishing to correct a defect when he knows it. We should add, for the strongest reason, a defect should never be flattered; we may say, also, that none should ever be neglected, whether it be serious or slight. A defect flattered, or even simply neglected, insensibly increases, and in the end becomes predominant. Then if it be serious, and of a certain nature, the consequences may be incalculable; the evil can no longer be arrested: we have some truly terrible examples of this kind. I will now mention two of these defects, which may easily become predominant when neglected; but I will here only point out to masters and young people those two domestic tyrants, which are the two plagues most to be feared at this age; I mean effeminacy and pride. Their ravages are really frightful; they tyrannize despotically over souls; they sometimes retain them in the most complete and disgraceful servitude. I shall refer to them again shortly and in detail. I shall now give the reason of the surprising predominance of certain defects in the soul; it is necessary to understand it well; it relates to the sources, even the deepest, of our nature; it is because since original sin there is not a bad germ in us, however trifling or pitiful it may be, which has not a tendency to increase, if it be not combated; which has not a tendency to take possession of all, rule all, corrupt all; while, on the contrary, there is no good disposition which has not a tendency to decay, if it be not cherished, and if we be not intent on strengthening it. And for this reason, also, we should never neglect a good disposition; a virtue, a grace, however trifling it may appear, if neglected, will perish. Hence so many vocations become lost, so many futures shipwrecked, because the first grace has been neglected. Vast subject! which of itself alone would furnish matter for the gravest instruction. Let us now enter into details.

CHAPTER IX.

CLASSIFICATION OF DEFECTS.

We do not mean to write a treatise on psychology or ethics here, and it is by no means our intention to give a philosophical and complete classification. We write for practical men, for masters, or rather for young minds, who have less need of a learned analysis of the human soul than of precise indications easy to be remembered. Without occuping ourselves to know whether, from a scientific point of view, the following division is correct, we simply say that the defects, whether positive or negative, may be classed, according to their kind, as corporal defects, intellectual defects, and moral defects.

Firstly, the corporal, physical, exterior defects. We consider it indispensable to describe them here, because they are of more importance than is generally supposed. What do I say? They may have the most serious influence in after-life on the success of the work which we shall be called on to perform. Education has not only a hold on such defects, but it can do much towards making them disappear, or at least considerably lessening them. We ought to mention that there are some to whom they cling during life, because they have never been admonished of them with courageous and enlightened charity. For example, apathetic dulness, coarse or awkward manners, a bad pronunciation, and many other defects of the same kind, may deprive us of the respect, confidence, and consideration required by us from many people, who can only know us through our exterior relations! And these are defects of which one can never rid himself, unless he labor to do so in good time. Again, for example — excuse such details — certain disagreeable infirmities, which one is himself ignorant of, a bad breath, a disagreeable odor from the feet, a want of neatness, and such like things, may inspire an unconquerable disgust for the most sensible and best-intentioned persons. There are precautions to be taken, and which people do not take, because they have not been warned of these defects and their remedies. How many times have I not seen persons, men of consideration, obliged to hold a council, in order to know how they might render acceptable to a friend an admonition on these points, so delicate and important, nevertheless so simple! Thus, again, a discordant voice, ridiculous gestures, a vulgar or harsh accent, may annul the effect of the most eloquently written and most learnedly composed sermon. I repeat it, there are defects that it is certainly useful to know; for then, if there be still time, they may be corrected. Nevertheless, how rarely is advice, even on these defects, however harmless they may be, gratefully received! And how few tender and devoted friends are to be found, even sensible directors, who will dare or think of admonishing on them! It is a great, and sometimes an immense, service to render. If it be so necessary to know even one's physical defects, how much more so is it to know the defects of one's mind, his intellectual defects! But, it must be said, it is here especially that every one is completely ignorant, or wishes to be ignorant, of himself. And, on the other hand, how difficult to find a sincere and courageous monitor for such defects! These defects are of different kinds, and more or less serious. For example, there is want of taste, which, in a writer or a preacher, will give to whatever he produces, though at the same time brilliant and solid, affectation, inflation, intemperance, oddity; in a word, may draw him into the most grievous and ridiculous errors. There is the want of judgment, especially practical judgment, errors of which, in the principal events of life, may cast a person into the falsest paths, precipitate him into enormous, and frequently irreparable, mistakes; in fine, causing him to wander, and make others, if it be his duty to direct them, wander at every step. And who will endure being warned of this defect, the only remedy for which can be the knowledge of it, and mistrust of self? There is the want of what is called wit, or rather the want of imagination. No doubt, it is not necessary to have an amount of wit or imagination; but it is indispensable that we should not think we have it when we have it not: for the sensible management of life, it is necessary to know how far a person is certain on this point; otherwise he will apply himself to matters for which he has not capacity, and in applying himself to them he will but lose his time, and accumulate follies.

There is the more serious want of penetration, elevation, extent of mind. This is a serious, but common, defect. With such a defect one can never be intrusted with certain work, certain important functions, certain delicate matters, without being exposed to taking false measures; narrowing, lowering, and perhaps stifling, the finest works. It is necessary at least that he distrust himself with reference to this, consequently know himself, and, in order to do that, suffer being admonished. There is, even in the mind, a certain want of sensibility, of which I will say a few words, because this defect is very serious, and prevents one on many occasions from accomplishing the most useful work, because he knows not the road to the heart, because he cannot adapt himself to the pleasures or the sorrows of others, and give timely encouragements or efficacious consolations. Well, there are these defects, and many others quite as serious, which it is as important to know, and of which no one, as we have already said, has the courage to inform us, because to inform a person of a mental defect wounds him to the quick.

There is scarcely one with which we can bear to be reproached, except want of memory; this we willingly enough acknowledge. With respect to all others, we do not know them, we do not wish to know them; whether it be through presumption, we believe ourselves capable of everything; whether it be through indolence, we do not wish to make any effort; in fine, whether it be through giddiness, we cannot listen to anything serious. I repeat, there is, nevertheless, hardly any of these defects, however profound they may be or appear to be, of which we cannot correct ourselves at least partly, or the disastrous consequences of which may not be prevented, if we have the happiness to be informed of them, the good sense to permit ourselves to be informed of them; the good will to attempt what we are capable of, so as to improve ourselves; and, finally, the modesty to keep to those works which can really lead to good.

But it may be said to me, Are there really efficacious remedies for these serious defects? Thanks to God, there are, and remedies almost infallible; and these are, humility and application.

There is hardly any one, however mediocre his mind may be, to whom we cannot say, Be humble, and have the intention, and you can do great things. Humility is not only supreme justice, but also supreme wisdom. It is not an easy matter to persuade vain and frivolous minds of this. Nevertheless, it can be done in education; and I have often seen it succeed. At present I know men, priests, who have become very useful, even distinguished; some of them occupy the first rank, who nevertheless were, and would have remained, of ordinary nature, but for the benefit derived from their education and the docility of their youth. Thanks to this double blessing, from ordinary natures they have yielded extraordinary fruits, supplied the deficiencies, developed their qualities, drawn from themselves all that God had placed in them, and, in this manner, have become elevated even above their nature: to-day they serve the church and society gloriously.

The moral defects, of which we have now to speak, are evidently the most serious; for, if they are not themselves actually sins, they are, at least, the sources of sin. Among these defects, there are some I will call natural, because they belong to the character, the nature, the spiritual, and sometimes even the physical, constitution of the individual; the others I will permit myself to designate the supernatural, because they are especially opposed to the virtues of grace, and are in man a most marked effect of the loss of original justice.[1]

The natural defects of a moral kind are very frequently founded in a quality which may become valuable, if the want of which it is the exaggeration, and of which it makes a deformity, be supplied. For example: a cool, discreet, reserved character sometimes appears concentrated and savage; nevertheless, experience has taught me that these characters frequently conceal under this apparent coolness a profound sensibility, and are capable of the truest and most devoted affection. What is necessary, then, in bringing them up, is to open and expand the heart, inspire them with a more overflowing sensibility, a mild and affectionate affability: there is

[1] In what sense, and from what point of view, I use the word "supernatural," may be seen; for I am not ignorant of, and by no means intend to contradict, the utterance of the Council of Trent, which declares man, by the sin of Adam, not only stripped of the gifts of grace, but wounded ever in the gifts of nature — *vulnerata in naturalibus.*

then found in such natures only a reserved delicacy, which, leaving itself to be divined, has but the more charms, — the gravity, dignity, composure, and precious dominion of the soul over itself. A firm character is prone to harshness; a lively character, to bluntness. If these defects be carefully corrected, there will remain of the firmness only activity and zeal.

There are some children who have what may be called a melancholy nature, a most tender heart, and a very reflecting mind. That is very dangerous — at least, unless the child should have good judgment, a firm character, and solid piety. Too reflecting a mind wearies the tender heart, grieves it: afterwards come the inevitable disappointments of life, the frictions; such a nature cannot bear them. What care the education of these children require! I have said, that, by the side of these defects, there is generally a good quality to be met with, of which they are the exaggeration and corruption: nevertheless, there are some of these natural defects which do not disguise any good quality; hence they are the more dangerous. A frivolous, vain, capricious, restless character produces disagreeable consequences, frequently even the most unhappy. Giddiness, inclination to chattering, and indiscretion, are, in every position, grievous, and sometimes very dangerous; but it can be easily imagined at what point, especially in a certain age and certain positions, these may become the source of the most serious inconvenience. Giddiness may cause a priest to forget the most sacred of his duties; gossiping and indiscretion are, on thousands of occasions, the causes of discord, and sometimes give birth to the most terrible misery. We can never make children comprehend sufficiently that the faults which they commit every day — trifling in themselves, perhaps — are not so if they consider the principles from which they arise, and the consequences that these evil principles may lead to; that the faults should be less regarded than the defects from which they proceed; that this defect which now, in their restricted life, causes them to commit small faults, will, later on, cause them to commit capital ones, if it remain in them; and remain it will, if they do not courageously attack and uproot it. It is by such considerations that the watchful severity of their masters should be justified in their eyes, and they induced to arm themselves with a generous will against their own defects.

I will say with respect to the correction of moral defects that which I said of intellectual defects: many, though they cling, like the latter, even to the nature of the individual, may also, like them, be corrected or diminished by constant practice of the virtues opposed to them; true humility knows how to discover them, and Christian perseverance in duty can uproot, or at least lessen, them. No; there is no man who cannot, by humility, and fidelity to duty, improve himself, and pursue a useful career; no weak character that cannot strengthen itself; no harsh character which cannot render itself endurable; no irascible character which cannot soften itself. But, to arrive at such desirable and uncommon results, how much zeal and light is necessary for those whose office it is to admonish, direct, and improve souls! How much docility is necessary for those who ought to accept advice, sometimes so painful to hear, though so important to be followed! All that we say respecting the zeal of masters and the docility necessary in children may be applied with particular truth in certain cases and to certain natures, among which want of harmony, of equilibrium, and the strongest contradictions, are to be met with. The degree to which this sometimes extends is wonderful. For example, we meet in a young man an inexplicable mixture of frivolity and seriousness, of vanity and sense, of mildness and harshness, of sight and blindness respecting himself, of nobility of soul and moral wretchedness, firmness of mind and weakness of character, rectitude of judgment, uprightness, and goodness of heart, with weakness of will, and insensibility of conscience, — natures whose contrasts stupefy the attentive observer, so much are they extraordinarily strong and extraordinarily weak, deep and frivolous, tender and suddenly dry and harsh, having a frankness sometimes admirable, nevertheless capable of such dissimulation that they seem to have the simplicity and composure of candor, a quick, clear, understanding, and a conscience so obscure that it appears to be extinct, a gratitude in which feeling and delicacy share the expressions, and which can suddenly give way to the most ungrateful appearances; again, no character more firm, or which assumes more pretension to courage, and at the same time more deficient in moral force.

Yes; in the course of my life I have often seen the want of harmony, I was about to say a divorce, between the different powers of the soul — the understanding, the heart, the will, the conscience; and this in the highest order of souls and natures. Yes, I have seen souls of the most uncommon, penetrating, spontaneous intelligence, even with a feeling and noble heart, capable of the most grievous failings and most painful errors; reason neither enlightening the heart nor the conscience, moral sense totally deficient, a great uprightness, a lively simplicity created for truth, a candor created for light, and all this suddenly wind up with lying; a heart profoundly tender, but this heart without light and strength, wavering in darkness, and this depth of sensibility becoming an abyss of misery. These natures are frightful; in spite of the superiority of mind and the dispositions of the heart, a deplorable moral deficiency may be met with, and consequently the greatest misfortunes occur during life. How important it is to study such natures, and do everything to assist them! But frequently the best education is not conducted in this manner. These contrasting natures weary and exhaust the masters: they do not know how to penetrate, to define, to govern them; few are capable of the intelligent, constant, study necessary for that; few have an eye sufficiently penetrating, a hand sufficiently pliant and strong. Also, how many times are they given up! how many times have I heard it said of these children, of these young people, in a dejected tone, "They are unaccountable"! Yes, but it is for you to define them, and to do everything in order to accomplish this end; it is for you to attend to them, to regard them closely, to beware of illusions, prejudices, and especially dejection; it is for you to remedy all this want of equilibrium, to harmonize all these contrasts, find out their deficiencies, take hold of their weak points, opposing their strength to their weakness, their resources to their defects, especially to enlighten those natures with respect to themselves; point out to them the danger; in fine, to determine the definitive preponderance of good qualities in them in such a direction as to conquer their defects. But for a work of this kind — for so difficult a cure — I will say piety is the indispensable auxiliary; it is piety only that can save souls in such great peril; piety alone can harmonize such natures — serve them as ballast and counterpoise, invincibly strengthen the understanding and the conscience, shelter the heart forever.

This is evidently one of the most delicate, most difficult matters in education. As to me, nothing has ever cost me more care and more trouble than the culture of these souls. Permit me to repeat here, in all its warmth and rude frankness, the speech which I one day addressed, with tender severity and merciless truth to one of them. These words were useful to his soul; they may be so to others likewise: "Of all the powers in your soul, understanding alone remains upright. But, strange as it may appear, the most singular rupture seems to have taken place between it, your conscience, and your heart. From this understanding, so clear, so quick, sometimes so luminous, light scarcely ever descends into conscience, causing it to say, with a firm and decisive judgment, This is good, this is evil. Again, still less light in this poor heart to make it love, sincerely love, what is good, what is amiable; to make it note, seriously note, what is bad, what offends God. This evident rupture of such an understanding with the conscience and the heart is something monstrous to view closely, as I have been obliged to do. It would make one wish himself blind, in order not to see the profound change, the singular abasement, as it were, a headlong descent of its natural elevation, in what remains of this understanding, this ardor, this uprightness, which is still so quick to recognize the truth. There is sometimes a shocking, even a gross, lowering of its primitive dignity, and that often to the most fantastic vulgarity. The moral levity of this poor intellect is still an enigma to me, and does not suffice to explain the blindness and impenetrable mystery of your conscience. You are aware I have given up fathoming it; I have receded before what St. Paul calls the mystery of iniquity — *mysterium iniquitatis.* The frightful serpent — the Liar — has passed there. Let me say more; he has sojourned in it. The ideas of good and evil, the principles of faith even, all have been disturbed — virtue, innocence, religion; it is difficult to say what this poor conscience firmly believes. But it must not be forgotten, that, if the measure of iniquity in your conscience has not been filled up until these latter days, the foibles, the defects, obscuring this conscience, have not ceased to increase since your ninth or tenth year, if I remember rightly what you told me of those early times. In a word, under pain of exposing yourself to the most frightful danger, and of seeing yourself, one day of your life, burst into the most unforeseen and irremediable scandals, you ought never to forget the terrible moral void, the disastrous deficiency, which, in this chief point, I have found in your soul. I repeat it, in my long career I have never seen anything which surprises me more, anything which leaves me more anxious, than your future. My hope is in your docility, your confidence, your firm and very faithful resolution, even to this day, of observing your rule, and of telling to those who direct you, not only your faults, but your defects, your whims, your contrasts, your deficiencies, such as this great and sad circumstance now makes known to you."

But let us leave for a moment these details; let us go still farther to the bottom of these matters; let us penetrate to the origin, even to the root, of these defects.

CHAPTER X.

PROFOUND ORIGIN OF OUR DEFECTS: ORIGINAL SIN: THE TRIPLE CONCUPISCENCE.

THE moral defects which we name supernatural, have more particularly, as we said in explaining this word, their source in original sin, and are, above all others, opposed to the more special virtues of grace; they form in us, we may say, a second nature, so deeply enrooted are they found to be. No one is entirely exempt from their taint, and it is the evil which lies deepest in our moral nature, since the heart of man has been corrupted. Assuredly the light which can most completely inform us, in this respect, ought to come from Him who knows, better than we do, all our disorders, and even the depths of sad humanity in in us. One of the most striking proofs of the divinity of the Holy Scriptures is the energy, the clearness, the profundity, with which the Bible reveals to us those of our vices which are the sources of all others. We admire there the eye of God, probing human nature with a piercing look, and discovering all that is deepest and most hidden in man. Here is what St. John the Evangelist says on this subject: *Omne quod est in mundo concupiscentia carnis est, et concupiscentia occulorum, et superbia vitæ.* These three phrases give the fullest explanation of the foundation of human affairs. Ancient philosophy, in the wisest of its sayings relating to the present question, has never pronounced anything to equal this simple verse of St. John. Without the light of these words, the moral world — entire humanity — would be an enigma. All the evils of human nature proceed from these three sources: nevertheless, there is one of the three that may be considered the most prolific, and to which all may be referred; it is pride — *superbia vitæ.* In addition to all the hideous and numerous offspring entirely its own, it is also, if we look closely into it, the father of the two other sources of evil indicated here. The Scripture itself, in another passage, teaches this sad and mysterious unity of the causes of our vices: *Initium omnis peccati superbia.*

However, in order thus to trace back every evil to pride, the most serious reflection, and sometimes very difficult research, are necessary; the explicit definition given by St. John of the three sources of all evil in us, — pride, sensuality, cupidity, — is, I say, most suitable to make every one comprehend how the defects and vices which afflict humanity arise. But it is a very remarkable fact, that, in these three profound words with which the evangelist sums up all the evil of the human heart, he addresses himself to young people, even to children, as well as grown men; because this concupiscence is in children and the young as well as in men; because children and young people are the men of the future; because childhood and youth are life in its germ. Hence in these young hearts are the seeds of all which should spring up and appear later on. It is, then, in this early age that the triple concupiscence should be combated, under pain of seeing it afterwards put forth terrible and vigorous shoots. But it must be also wrestled with during our whole life. It is for this reason St. John calls all ages to this work—fathers, as well as sons; masters at the same time as their pupils; old men, as well as young men, and children themselves. He addresses himself to all, without exception: to fathers, *scribo vobis, patres;* to young men, to youths, to children, *vobis juvenes, adolescentes, infantes.* And St. John himself gives his reason for thus specially appealing to youth, because it is the age of generous zeal, of valiant strife: *Scribo vobis, adolescentes, quia vicistis malignum*—"I write to you, young men, because you have conquered the enemy and the evil." *Scribo vobis, juvenes, quoniam fortes estis*—"I write to you, young men, because you are strong." Yes; in spite of the degeneracy of the age, Christian youth is strong; it has in it a divine source of strength and virtue, of which the apostle says, *Et Verbum Dei manet in vobis*—"And the Word of God dwells in you." Behold why Christian youth is strong: it has in it the Word of God, the revealed lights and inspirations of faith; and through these divine virtues it triumphs over the Evil Spirit—*et vicistis malignum!*

You, then, who bring up the rising generation, and who also have in you the Word of God, the supernatural strength of faith and grace, call Christian youth, and guide it to the holy strife, to the struggle against the enemy, against evil, against the triple concupiscence, — all the success of its education depends upon that. I have already said, and I repeat it, whosoever does not know, that, in the great work of education, it is against the triple concupiscence he must struggle, knows nothing, does nothing. Owing to their foundation, the principles of education partake of the same idea with the highest Christian ethics, which always point out this triple concupiscence as the eternal enemy of the soul and of salvation, and teach that it must be unceasingly mortified, crucified, bound to the three branches of the Cross; thus proving that the great doctrine of Christian mortification, which is the main point of the medicinal morality of the Gospel, is also the sinew of all real education. And here, again, the words of St. Paul become admirably verified: *Pietas ad omnia utilis est* — "Piety is useful for all things." It is on this account, that, in a house of Christian education, so much importance is attached to piety. Let us now enter into all the details of this sad and important subject.

CHAPTER XI.

PRIDE, SUPERBIA VITÆ, THE CHIEF SOURCE OF OUR DEFECTS.

I.

Pride; its Nature.

PRIDE, the principal and most fruitful of deadly sins, occupies a sad and wide space in human life. No vice extends its empire farther. It is to be met with in all men, all ages, all states of life. It blends with everything; it invades every place; it is the universal evil. As Bossuet admirably says, "It is this vice which has flowed into the depths of our interior with the words of the serpent, who said to us, in the person of Eve, 'You will be as gods' — *eritis sicut dii.* We have swallowed this mortal poison; it has penetrated even to the marrow of our bones, and our whole soul is infected with it."[1] Again, it is the temptation of every creature. The dream of pride in every soul is to ascend — in his mind, in his heart, in his life; to exalt itself, to intoxicate itself, with its own excellences. Pride is, then, at the same time, the oldest malady of our nature, and the most dangerous wound that the ancient enemy of mankind could have given us; and he has given it of a

[1] Treatise on Concupiscence, chap. x.

frightful depth to the hearts of all. Besides, this is the vice which breaks out soonest in us. There are some that lie dormant in children for a greater or less length of time; pride, on the contrary, develops itself in them at an early age, and sometimes to an extraordinary degree. There are some children, already at ten years of age or even sooner, literally prodigies of pride. Sad to say, virtue itself is not safe from its taint; like a gnawing worm, pride glides secretly into the purest hearts, spoiling and corrupting the best actions, the finest virtues. We sometimes meet souls who would be great, who would be noble, who have love and zeal for the good, the beautiful; but pride, which is at the bottom of these souls, breathes over them a mischievous blast which blights all their charms.

Plato somewhere says, "The greatest evil of man is a defect that is born with him, which every one excuses in himself, and, consequently, which no one ever labors to rid himself of; it is what is called self-love." Plato knew well how to point out this evil; but to indicate the remedy, and especially to make acceptable the radical treatment of so profound an evil, is what neither Plato nor any one could ever do. *Hoc Plato nescivit*, says St. Jerome. Jesus Christ has done it, and it is in this He has shown Himself to be God: "Learn of me to be meek and humble of heart." Admirable words! We see here the Divine Physician at once putting his hand precisely on the evil place, and applying the remedy to the sharpest wound of our nature. We shall soon speak of all these hideous vices which pride gives birth to in the soul.

Nevertheless, nothing is more difficult to be observed and well defined than pride, because its fecundity is prodigious, and its disguises and artifices are innumerable. Sensual from its foundation, it has its subtleties and its cunning — sometimes the most unheard-of refinements; it conceals, transforms itself: it is at once the most prolific and most deceitful of defects; it almost always clothes itself in appearances which are but so many wiles. Thus pride appears firm and high, and it is most frequently weak, low, frivolous, restless. It appears noble and great, and at bottom is base, even coarse. *Superbia non est magnitudo, sed tumor*, says St. Augustine. Yes, with its immoderate pretensions, it has incredible littleness; with its false and vain greatness, it falls into arrant meanness. Strange! with all its artifices, it tends to delude and dupe itself especially; it wishes to impose on others, and most frequently deceives only itself. By a just chastisement, it finds shame where it wished unduly to find glory. It is because pride is actually, when we examine it to the bottom, when we scrutinize well its nature, founded on a lie; it is injustice, it is even lying. *In veritate non stetit*, say the Scriptures, in speaking of the first of the proud, and the prince of pride. But what, then, is pride? Pride, says the catechism — we cannot do better than borrow from its numerous definitions — is an esteem and ill-regulated love of self, which causes one to prefer himself to others, and relate everything to self, and nothing to God. That is evidently supreme injustice in a being who is nothing and has nothing of himself; or, rather, who has of himself only miseries too real by the side of the advantages he has received from God, and which he arrogates to himself as if they came from him. It is an arrogant and indecent forgetfulness of the foundation of his being, which is all borrowed, and remains in everything and always dependent on God. To God alone belongs all glory; He owes it to Himself, He gives it to Himself. He demands it; it is due to Him; and to wish it for self is to wish for what does not belong to self; it is to ravish from God that which He alone merits; it is to commit a robbery, a real sacrilege. Pride must be very unjust, and much out of place, in a created and dependent being, since, according to the clever and sensible remark of Fénelon, "pride is obliged to conceal itself, and can only escape public derision by seeming to forget itself." To be actually glorious is to be vain. Glory is only admired whilst it is concealed, and he who displays it is odious and despised. Let the man of the world, otherwise most admirable, openly demand to be admired; let him ingenuously display his glory—he becomes the plaything of those whose admiration he would have if he did not ask it. What, then, is this affair so disproportioned to the condition of man that he cannot be forgiven for pretending openly to it? Such a pretension feels in itself the need of dissimulation; falsehood, which is so odious and contemptible in every other matter, is the only means of making pride endurable; and the simplicity, which is everywhere else amiable, becomes here odious and ridiculous. It is because pride is not in its place in the creature; it is because every one instinctively feels that it is there misplaced and unjust. And again, on this account, it is, and appears, indecent. Yes, there is a decency, because there is a justice, in modesty, in humility; and there is an indecency in pride, because there is an injustice and a usurpation in it. Modesty is the bashfulness of the soul; pride is the incontinence of it. A proud soul is a soul which no longer contains itself. Hence the affinities of concupiscence of the mind, of pride, with shameful concupiscence. Modesty, purity of soul and body, consists in containing itself, in maintaining the dignity of self. Pride, vanity, self-love, like immodesty, consists in not containing itself, not respecting itself, in flattering, in miserably worshiping self. Pride is, then, the ostentation, the immodesty, the impudence, the incontinence, of the mind; as impurity is the impudence, the immodesty, the incontinence, and in a manner the pride, of the the body. Pride is likewise a shameful vice; it must be blushed for like the others; one may feel the temptations of both in spite of himself, but he must blush for them. And for this reason it is a vice so abhorred and odious. Pascal has said, "Self is hateful;" self, that is to say, the pride which sees but self, thinks but of self, which is occupied only with self, which refers everything to self. God and men have a horror of it; and the punishments which God reserves for it prove how culpable it is; they are sometimes frightful. It is related that a thunderbolt, having one day secretly struck a column in a church, kindled there a hidden fire, which in course of time became a terrible conflagration, and ended by leading to a dreadful fall: thus it is with the chastisements of pride, — they are often strokes of lightning. Pride is in itself its own terrible chastisement; the haughty soul is sufficiently punished through the evils that pride gives birth to, through the vices of which it is the father. We are now going to say a few words on this subject.

II.

The sad Fecundity of Pride.

There is really cause for being frightened when we consider the long train of defects, vices, and crimes, which pride engenders. Nevertheless, it is right and necessary to study, and cause to be closely studied, this grievous spectacle. It is the best means of inspiring in young people hatred of a vice which is but too much allied with the frivolity and presumption of their age, and to give them the energy and courageous will indispensable for combating and triumphing over it. Whosoever believes himself pure from all pride deludes himself greatly. There is a very simple and safe proceeding by which one can recognize this vice in himself or others: let him regard the conduct and the acts; let him examine if he cannot discover some fruit of this pride; it is easily seen: most certainly, then, the root is there, and deep and flourishing in proportion as the fruits are more abundant and more evil. Firstly, disobedience, that is to say, the want of submission to the orders of lawful superiors, or revolt against the direction and advice of those whose office it is to guide us;

from whence does it proceed, if not from pride? One wishes to have only his own will for rule; he believes himself superior to every one, and perfectly capable of governing himself; hence he counts as nothing the wisest and most legitimately established authority. In a house of education it is the overthrow of all rule, all discipline, all respect. Education essentially supposes docility. It is evident that a child, a young man, has need of being guided. No man has every light, every experience, all sense, of himself alone; but especially a young man — what light, what experience, what knowledge, can he have? No: whosoever in early age believes himself capable of directing himself, is averse to submission, rebels against obedience, is manifestly tainted with an intolerable pride, of which, alas! he will be the first victim. Teachers of youth, impress well on your pupils that it is necessary, during the whole of life, to distrust self, to accept advice, to respect authority. Never has the following speech come from the mouth of a sensible man, "I know what I have to do, and do not need the advice of any one;" but when a young man, a child, uses this language, it is a great pity and a great misfortune. No doubt, in a house of education, indocility and disobedience may come from giddiness; we should then be more indulgent in its repression. But when they proceed, as most frequently happens, from pride, oh! an inflexible firmness is necessary, and especially to attack this disobedience in its source, that is to say, in pride. Let us not forget that it is always pride that must be striven with in disobedient children. Pride has still many other consequences: violent passions, hatreds, sometimes ferocious revenges, usually have hardly any other origin than pride. In an inferior degree, it engenders envy, that is to say, the base sorrow one feels at the well-being of his neighbor; jealousy, which drives him to the wish of dispossessing him of his wealth, in order to enjoy it in his place, and torments him with regret for remaining deprived of it. Pride likewise inspires one with pleasure at the misfortunes of another, a secret intention to injure him, scandal, and calumnies; these are so many hateful impulses of the heart against every superiority that wounds and humiliates us; it is, at least, a malignant delight in what procures the abasement of others, and in that way seems to elevate us. Every time that a man discovers in his heart, or the heart of others, any one of these evil shoots, he may be certain that pride is there; bitter root of bitter fruit: *Radix amaritudinis.* When this pride has another offensive passion, such as the eager love of gain, of money, as an auxiliary, the amount of self-forgetfulness, insolence, ingratitude, or crimes, it may inspire, is incredible. The portrait of envy, of jealousy, has many times been drawn, *Là git la sombre envie, a l'œil timide et loucheté;* they can never be depicted so base, so odious, as they really are, especially in youth; for they have much less right to be among young people than among men. They become particularly wretched; they destroy sincere and pure friendships, they pervert and poison noble and fruitful emulation; they substitute for the generous sentiments of this age a bitter gall, a sharp rancor; they narrow hearts that would require expansion; they depress souls which would need elasticity. Besides, it is difficult to attack this unhappy passion directly, because it dissimulates as long as it can; nothing is more vile in the heart, nothing more painful to point out. How, then, combat it? To souls debased in this manner by a sad pride it is necessary to show all the nobleness of a brave emulation, the sweetness of a loyal friendship, and the duty of great Christian charity. It is necessary to inspire them with kindness of heart also; for pride is the great enemy to kindness of heart. Pride is positively wicked. It is hard, tyrannical, violent, cruel. It needs a victim, which it torments for its pleasure. It loves stinging raillery, mockery, sarcasm; it delights in tears; as it increases, it will love blood. I have said somewhere that children are naturally wicked; it is especially of proud children that this must be said. Children in whom pride predominates do not respond to affection; they refer everything to themselves; they admire nothing; they do not love: if they sometimes appear to love a master, it is because this master flatters them. They seem to love their parents, but only while they receive presents from them. In truth, they are profoundly ungrateful. It is necessary to speak to them frequently of the great and beautiful virtue of gratitude — to make them sensible of the nobleness, the sacred duty of it; to brand before them ingratitude; to point out to them the baseness, the disgrace, and the blackness of it sometimes. On all that they must be spoken to plainly, without sparing them; I would even say it is necessary not to use delicacy. Experience has taught me that such children have no delicacy, and, grossly blind to themselves, they do not understand it. Let us continue this sorrowful enumeration. The desires, the ardent dreams, of greatness, of glory, of renown, more precocious, more frequent, than is supposed among children, in a word, foolish ambition, also reveal a heart given up to pride. He whose mind relishes the name of learned, of great orator, of great man; he who dreams of pompous titles, ideas of honors, of brilliant dignities, in his future, — may, without fear of error, be warned that he should suspect himself of pride. The danger of such dreams is great beyond measure. These desires soon dissolve, leaving in the heart a depth of grievous vexation or blind hatred, which at least poisons life, and frequently breaks out in a terrible manner. In the sad times which we live in, this disposition of mind is particularly dangerous. The impulse which has precipitated so many young souls into anti-social Utopias has very often had for starting-point and origin the disappointments of a precocious, ardent, and mistaken ambition. Perspicacious masters, those who do not rest on their present foresight, but think of the future, should regard it very attentively. Again, it is very necessary to mention anger — impetuous emotion of the soul, which prompts it to repulse with violence all that displeases it. Abuse and imprecations, daughters of anger, are the outbursts of a pride which can no longer be cautious, which becomes exasperated against that which wounds it, and seeks at every expense a brutal superiority. Likewise all these defects, which sometimes so sadly disfigure the best dispositions, and suddenly place, as it were, a veil of ugliness over the face of the child who gives himself up to them, — pouting, murmuring, impoliteness, churlishness, insolent answers, — what are they but the proud rebellion of a mind which considers itself above propriety, and does not wish to acknowledge its errors or weaknesses? and what is more common in a house of education? How many children lose the fruit of their excellent qualities, draw upon themselves bitter anger, merited reprimands, and, what is much worse, prepare for themselves in real life a deplorable future! Vanity, which is an ill-regulated desire for esteem and praise; ostentation, which prompts us to display the wealth and talents we possess; presumption, which gives us too conceited an idea of ourselves, and causes us to say more than becomes us, undertake more than we can perform; haughtiness, arrogance, even ill-temper, — are the well-known daughters of pride. A clear-sighted master will immediately point out to him who falls into these different faults the vice with which he is tainted. But that which young people do not sufficiently know, and have great need of knowing, is the fatal consequences of all these defects, born of pride. For example, how many things, at the least ridiculous, and frequently dangerous and culpable, do not vanity and ostentation cause young people, and even men, to do and say! Again, to speak only of the vain searching after adornment, the imprudent indiscretion of speech among young people — from whence do they come? Will you say that the exaggerated care of his toilet and of his person is but frivolity, and of no great consequence in a young man? Such would be a serious error. It is something more than the indication of an empty head and little mind. All those who have experience of young people know that virtue itself, in all that is most essential to it, is compromised by these miserable futilities, which develop in a young man tastes, habits of mind and character, incompatible with the generous energy, the solid sense, and bashful reserve, without which virtue cannot be maintained.

It is for this reason that Fénelon, who saw clearly the danger of it in youth, did not fail to anticipate and attack this species of vanity and foolish pride. He says, "It is true, we may seek neatness, suitability, and decency in the clothes necessary for covering our bodies; but, after all, these stuffs which cover us can never become a vain and affected ornament. A young man who loves to adorn himself foolishly, like a woman, is unworthy of wisdom and glory." The faults which ostentation and the frivolous desire of making one's self valuable cause, during life, are innumerable. Blinded, and at the same time intoxicated, one loses his discernment; he no longer understands the bearing of words; he does not suspect their snares; he compromises himself, delivers himself up to them, — he loses himself.

Fénelon, that great master, who has so profoundly fathomed all the recesses of the heart, understood well the gravity of this danger for young people; and we are sensible, from the manner in which he speaks of it, how much he had been struck by it. There is an admirable passage of his, which I have frequently brought under the notice of my pupils, and in which this peril is pointed out with surprising perspicacity: "Seduced by adroit praise, the son of Ulysses allowed himself to go on making a long recital of his adventures, and in this recital he told all; he could not be silent on anything; hence he cast himself into frightful danger, which his master saw well, but of which he himself had not even the slightest idea. As soon as they were alone, Mentor hastened to make him observe it. 'The pleasure of recounting your adventures,' said he to him, 'has carried you away; you have charmed the goddess in explaining to her the dangers from which your courage and industry have drawn you; hence you have only prepared for yourself a more dangerous captivity. The love of vain-glory has caused you to speak without prudence. She has engaged you in recounting these histories, to learn from you what has been the fate of Ulysses; she has found means of speaking a long time without saying anything; and she has drawn you into explaining to her all she wished to know: such is the art of a flattering and impassioned woman. When, O Telemachus! will you be sufficiently wise never to speak through vanity, and when will you know how to keep silent on all that is profitable to you when it is not beneficial to speak? Another time, learn to speak more soberly of all that can attract praise for you.'"

I have not yet said anything of susceptibility, which does not, like vanity or ostentation, seek for praise, but which becomes offended with the slightest reproach, the least suspicion; it is a false tenderness for one's self which denotes scarcely less of pride. There are some children, some natures, which are truly sensitive; we cannot give them a warning, address to them a reprimand, or the mildest advice, without their becoming grieved, shocked, or irritated. At the least word from a schoolfellow or a master you will see them redden or grow pale. We feel that there is in them a chord on which the hand must not be put; a tender spot which must not be touched even with the point of the finger. The education of children with such a disposition is much to be dreaded, and the correction of their faults is rendered extremely difficult. We can only arrive at reclaiming young natures so susceptible by prudently and mildly urging them on to the end. There is still another species of minds among whom the susceptibilities of pride are somewhat singular. They are men who seem to be in the world only to save appearances. They value but the stamp. Frivolous at heart, serious only in the exterior, they can judge gravely, but only surface-deep; people whose character, through their weakness and fanaticism for decorum, becomes lowered by the glance of an eye. This, again, is a grievous kind of pride. Lying, which disguises a painful truth; cupidity, which is never satisfied with what it has; and especially harshness to the little and poor, to servants, to every one with whom we have dealings and who are beneath us, and a thousand other defects of this kind, may be all referred to pride. Everywhere it is love of self, egotism; it is self which rules; self to which all is sacrificed; self which is adored. Hypocrisy, which wishes to conceal under a mantle of honor the shameful passions that devour it, is also a daughter of pride. The proud hypocrite is, of all, the most to be dreaded. Again, it must be said that pride is the father of incredulity, apostasy, impiety; this is, alas! too well known. If a man no longer believes in religion, or pretends to no longer believe in it, it is from one of two causes, — either because he elevates his weak reason above everything, he worships it; or more frequently, especially in youth, he gives way to the petty vanity, still more contemptible, of wishing to distinguish himself from the crowd, and appear strong-minded. *Quomodo potestis credere*, says our Lord, *vos qui gloriam ab invincem accipitis?* Profound and terrible words of Him who scrutinizes the thoughts and hearts of men.

In a house of Christian education, doubts against faith are frequently enough caused by pride and vanity, or the cowardliness of human respect. As soon as a young man becomes proud, you may be certain his faith is in jeopardy; and, if you wish to save his faith, hasten to use a remedy for pride. This incredulity through pride, pitiful even in a grown man, is truly a misery without name in a young man, who knows nothing, and can know nothing; who imagines that he contains more wisdom in his little head than the greatest minds of the world, who have believed with pleasure. It is, more especially, this foolish incredulity of the young that Bossuet strikes with terrible ridicule: "What have they seen, these uncommon geniuses?" In fine, it must be said that impurity, though it may be the immediate fruit of effeminacy, is also very often the fruit of pride, *through chastisement.*

God punishes pride, in delivering it up to ignominious passions. *Tradidit illos in passiones ignominiæ,* says St. Paul. Experience offers proofs of this, as unexceptionable as sorrowful. A director of souls, a priest charged with bringing up youth, cannot be ignorant of this great danger from pride. When he sees pride increase in a child, in a young man, otherwise pious and regular, let him tremble for this menaced virtue, and let him warn him of it; terrible falls are not far off, if pride be persisted in. Such is, in part — for we have not spoken of all, we cannot speak of all — the fatal and disgraceful generation of defects that pride gives birth to. The chief point is to know all that well; for it is the key to the science of morals. Pride is the most profound, the most ancient, the most universal, the most grievously fruitful, malady of our fallen nature; it is the generating principle of evil in us. To be ignorant of it, or to know it but imperfectly, would necessarily have the most fatal consequences. But to know it in an abstract manner is not sufficient; not to recognize in one's self this vice, and its ramifications so multiplied, the unmentionable detail of faults of which it is, every moment in life, the unhappy origin, would be a deplorable blindness. Pride is so fertile in poisons for our poor mind and our sad heart, we may say with truth, that humility alone — its antidote — could restore good sense and virtue to human nature.

However long the enumeration we are making may already be, it is, nevertheless, very incomplete; nothing less than an entire moral treatise, embracing the highest questions of psychology, society, family, religion, even of politics, would be necessary to complete it. However, before leaving this subject, we wish to speak again of the four kinds of evil spirits that pride is the source of, and one or other of which frequently stains the best composed characters, the purest virtues, and, in a house of Christian education, the most pious children.

CHAPTER XII.

ON THE FOUR KINDS OF EVIL SPIRITS WHICH PRIDE IS FATHER TO.

THE first of these is the spirit of indocility. Indocility is not disobedience; it is more and less. A child can be very indocile in obeying. Indocility (in the sense of the Latin word, *indocilis,* which does not permit of explanation) means that one is full of confidence in his own lights, and has no confidence in the lights of others. He has no faith in any one. He respects not the mind, the authority, of any one. Indocility is still less in the exterior act than in the interior disposition, in the mind and in the heart; for this reason the Scripture says, *Cor malum incredulitatis.*

The immediate inconvenience of this spirit of indocility is to deprive the indocile young man of the lights of those who, by their knowledge, wisdom, experience, and devotion, are called to be his guides; of leaving him to walk alone and unsupported, exposed to all the falls which his vanity and inexperience will not fail to meet occasions of; and causing him to waste, in unprofitable attempts or ruinous trials, time or faculties, the fruits of which would have been, perhaps, otherwise precocious and certain. And, hence, what misfortunes later in life!

what a source of numberless faults, and how important to prevent these misfortunes by docility in youth! how many talents become sterile, how many become even fatal, how many happy natures pine away, how many fall into evil, in consequence of this secret pride, which renders them indocile to the lessons of authority, experience, superiority, devotion, and closes beforehand every path to wise advice! for who will venture on exposing himself to give advice, the inutility of which he foresees? Well, I should say this terrible indocility is the great evil of Christian youth.

The youth of the age is grossly disobedient; pious youth is sometimes profoundly indocile. Innate pride is to be found among all men under the form of self-esteem, disguised, perhaps, but deep-seated, and which gives birth to a surprising spirit of resistance. It is the chief point to understand in education; and a man should not make education his occupation if he does not understand that.

The second kind of spirit that we wish to point out, as a consequence of pride, is the spirit of independence. This is not, like the preceding one, attachment to one's own lights; it is attachment to one's own will; a very subtle defect, clever at disguising itself, even under a virtuous exterior. There is something flattering for a soul in being able to say of itself, "What I will, I will firmly." Without doubt, that is fine; but it may serve to conceal the most unreasonable obstinacy and an unbridled pride. A person is not firm because he does not yield even to the reasonable and lawful will of others, and because he wishes to make his own will triumphant everywhere; he is but stiff-necked and imperious. Besides, this pretended firmness frequently conceals a real weakness; it is evident more strength is necessary for ruling one's self, and bending spontaneously to reasonable advice, in spite of the conquering resistances of pride, than hardening one's self in a vain and foolish haughtiness. It is a great misfortune for all society when this spirit of independence prevails, when no one can give up his own will in order to place himself under that of others. Nothing is more specially dangerous than to bring such a spirit into the Church. It is, nevertheless, the evil of the age; and, sad to say, — what should arouse the most serious attention of the directors of seminaries, — ecclesiastics themselves are not exempt from it; it is the air we breathe, and in which we live; one is naturally more independent to-day, at twenty years of age, than he was at fifty under Louis XIII. Whosoever is still ignorant of this disposition of the youth of our day is not capable of being beneficial to it. But it is for skilled Christian education to re-act energetically against this detestable spirit, which now breathes everywhere, and, more or less, inspires all youth; it is for education to combat with and replace it by the noble and generous docility which so well becomes young people, especially those formed in the school of religion.

The spirit of contradiction is the third kind of evil spirit engendered by pride. It is a whim; a most disagreeable mania. The spirit of contradiction renders a man unendurable to every one. There are some minds so constructed, nothing can be said before them that they will not support the opposite of it; they would believe themselves without character if they agreed with the opinions of others. Sometimes it is an inexpressibly mistaken love of truth, an unseasonable frankness, a puerile simplicity, which never sees the inconvenience of speaking its mind; it is still more frequently a secret pride and a foolish self-sufficiency. Such minds believe themselves obliged to contradict at once everything that does not agree with their views; they become infatuated in their ideas, and we see them unceasingly, with a ridiculous pertinacity, become stubborn in interminable and sterile discussions. Nevertheless, into what errors are they not frequently drawn from having embraced, without knowing well why, and only for the sake of contradiction, some opinion which afterwards they have not the courage to abandon! This mania of contradiction is most frequently caused by a little mind puffed up with pride.

A superior man, with a truly noble heart, does not hesitate, as soon as he perceives his error, to adopt boldly an opinion, the justness of which he had not, at first, quite seen, though, by so doing, he should lose the opportunity of displaying his resources in discussion, and condemn himself to silence. In any case, he will never dispute for the love of disputing, and he will have the politeness, as well as good sense, to allow many things to pass which there would be more inconvenience in raising than in neglecting.

To find a name for the fourth kind of spirit produced by pride, we are obliged to call it — if we may use the expression — the spirit of justification. It is the mania of always justifying one's self; of excusing one's self, ever and anon, right or wrong; of never being willing to admit a fault: *volens justificare se ipsum;* like the Pharisee in the Gospel. There are some young people whom we can never bring to admit their most evident faults; they will say they believe themselves impeccable; and if they fall into any material, flagrant faults, impossible to be denied, they are always perfectly innocent in intention. Their first thought, as soon as we make a remark to them or approach them, is to seek any excuse whatsoever, and afterwards they stick obstinately to it. They are right beforehand; they do not even examine if what is said to them has a foundation; they combat it all at once. Nothing betrays more of secret pride than such a disposition, and, I will even say, nothing is more calculated to set the mind astray and narrow the heart. A just mind, aided by a good, simple, honest heart, will seek out the true side of a reproach, and what foundation there is for a remark; hence it will acquire valuable knowledge of itself, and at the same time it will, by this simplicity, show itself superior even to its fault. On the contrary, the mind which I speak of, full of pride and vanity, closes its eyes on all that is most certain and most evident in its faults, and becomes ingenious in imagining reasons for its exculpation; such is its chief solicitude, its first impulse, — a sure indication of a little mind and a barren heart. It is very important to make young people, tainted with this grievous malady, understand well that this sad spirit of justification is everything that is most miserable; and, on the contrary, how honorable and glorious is the plain, noble avowal of a fault. The first thing that an upright and sincere young man ought to acknowledge is, that at no age are we more exposed to be mistaken in a thousand ways than in youth; and, consequently, at no age, also, should we be more disposed to allow ourselves to be reprehended and admonished.

CHAPTER XIII.

A LAST WORD ON THE MANNER OF TREATING THE PROUD.

CERTAINLY we do not think we have spared pride; and after what we have said — though we may not have said all — if pride did not appear to an upright young man supremely dangerous and hateful, it would be because this vice still exercised over his heart a very powerful fascination. Yet it must not be forgotten, that, in education, the obstacles may become the means, and that it shows the talent, and is the duty, of the person educating, to convert the obstacles into the means. Self-love, perilous as it is, may itself become a valuable auxiliary. It is a devious power, but it is a power; it is less necessary to break it than to direct it. Self-love always tends to flatter and exalt those of whom it has possession; but sometimes these excesses themselves are evidences of a generous nature, capable of ascending very high, if pride did not frequently cause it to descend so low. What is necessary, then, is, not to stifle this generosity of nature, this haughtiness of soul, but to take possession of and rule it. It deceives itself, not in its aim, but in its object. Two things are necessary to draw it away from the wretchedness in which it is being caught and lost, and turn it towards an object worthy of it — towards its real object; to give it its food; point out its end; in fine, to take possession of it for good and great deeds. There are, then, two ways of treating self-love, — it must be checked at first, and then roused; its errors must be repressed, and its energies directed. This work is often very delicate, and it is not, and cannot be, performed in the same way for all children. Here, as is always the case, the complex and varied nature of children requires to be closely observed; the means of repression or encouragement should be well adapted to the characters.

There is a self-love that it is necessary to know how to spare, to watch, to wait for, to seize only at a favorable opportunity, and to attack, but with great precaution; there is a self-love that must be striven with in front, and without sparing; stricken as soon as it displays itself, and humiliated even to the dust. The first is to be met with among weak, feeling, delicate characters, without great vigor or elasticity. A direct, harsh, merciless humiliation would dishearten and break them; a paternal reprimand, a friendly advice, firm and mild, a lesson full of instruction, will humble them, but will permit them to raise themselves again. The other species of self-love is to be met with among energetic and strong characters, and it starts up with insolence; the suddenness, the harshness, of the punishment makes them bow down the head, without, however, taking away their elasticity and their courage. Nevertheless, even there, and in the just severity of the most rigorous reprimand, it is necessary to let them see that it is with the pride, and not the person, that we contend; otherwise they will not listen to anything; they will become hardened. These strong natures are frequently accessible to tenderness; harsh, violent, without regard, and without respect, while they obey pride, they will recover, when pride is conquered, and when urged by an affectionate word, their natural goodness.

There is here again, as always, the favorable moment to be seized; the fitting time is necessary in point of correction more than in every other matter. Self-love, which is so afflicting in education, so delicate to manage, so difficult to correct, presents otherwise, I have said, occasions of which it is easy to make great use. This fiery nature may not accept a reproach, and, indeed, may start into a passion when you wish to repress it. Well, without ever weakening or softening, seek for and find the opportunity of animating it by praise. The power of a commendation suitably given, with limits and delicacy, is sometimes surprising. I have known a child so full of vanity, so filled with himself, so impatient of correction and of obedience, that, at the least remark or command from his tutor, it was rare when he did not reply at once with insolence. The tutor, who had a firm hand, chastised him on the moment, by a word terrible for impassibility and truth, with a calm but inflexible measure; nevertheless, he gained much more, he managed him much more easily, when praise had been able to anticipate the reprimand — when, during the morning, he had been able to find any occasion whatsoever, sometimes *apropos* of nothing, to make him, with moderation, a merited compliment. Fénelon recognizes not only advantages in, but the necessity of, treating children thus, and he recommends giving them at proper times suitable encouragement. "If," says he, "we never praise children when they do well, we run the risk of disheartening them. Though it may be feared praise causes vanity, it is necessary to try and make use of it to animate children without intoxicating them. We see that St. Paul frequently employs it to encourage the weak, and to make correction pass more mildly. The Fathers have made the same use of it. It is true, that, to render it beneficial, it must be seasoned in such a manner as to take away the exaggeration, the flattery, of it, and at the same time refer all good to God, as the source of it."

Pride is, then, a passion that may be skilfully governed, not by yielding to it, but in a manner deceiving it by cleverly and calculatingly caressing it, as we caress a fiery horse with the hand in order to restrain and calm him. Again, pride is a passion that it is possible to convert into a noble emulation and generous eagerness. It is necessary to incite youth to good and great deeds; to fill it with enthusiasm and admiration; for that, it is important to know what gives pleasure to these young and ardent souls, and win them by means of that which they love. In general, children are scarcely sensible of, and have little admiration for, cold and solid parts. But extraordinary, heroic, valiant deeds please them; battles, missions, martyrs, great conversions of souls, excite their admiration; and this enthusiasm is beneficial; for this reason it is of consequence to prompt them to it; when they find this noble aliment for the fire of their hearts, it is no longer immersed in wretchedness. Feats of strength, agility of body, dexterity at games, victory in racing, also fascinate them. All these are good, without danger, and consequently may be used, and become excellent as diverting remedies. In short, there is an art in training self-love, in checking it, and even in making use of it, to lead to good. When one finds himself in face of a proud, indocile, disrespectful nature, let him calmly, persistently, zealously study every form of that pride; all its tints, all its sallies, all its whims, all its shadows; let him watch attentively every moment; let him apply with firmness and prudence every remedy. Such natures are rarely sterile for good; they may give way to terrible excesses, but they are also capable of great deeds. There is in these souls a seed of generosity, and it is a great resource; this seed is damaged, impaired, and, out of the abundance of its sap, puts forth insolent and haughty shoots; but the sap is there, the germ is there; it must be purified, ennobled; then wonderful fruits may spring up; and it is the duty of education to do everything in order to produce them.

As a termination to this long chapter, permit me to place here, in its first crudeness and warmth, a note given by me to a very young professor, carried away and unknowingly ruined by pride, and who, frightened by the danger he was in, one day sincerely asked me to tell him the whole truth respecting his pride, and to spare him in nothing. I sent to him the following lines, which he had the courage to receive and meditate on, and which were of great benefit to his soul. "There is," I wrote to him, "a great wound in your soul — a deep wound which unceasingly enlarges. You sometimes forget it, but it is there, and it threatens to invade everything in your soul — all your ideas, all your sentiments, all your affections. There is in you a love towards yourself of unmeasured strength; it is a something unrestrained which rules and transports you, often unknown to you. Nevertheless, most frequently the wish to know yourself would be sufficient; but you prefer illusion. You have a horror of being irritated by your fellow-professors or your superior; the slightest admonition irritates you, raises your indignation to an extraordinary point; it is frightful to see. I have sometimes been deeply grieved to the heart by it. To-day, I thank God, you seek for His light; but you are usually not in earnest, you do not wish to be enlightened. You delude yourself on defects that you find intolerable in others. You hold on to your strict duty only by a tie almost forced. Your love for yourself inspires in you a secret hate of the authority of others, and makes you exercise your own with an inflexible harshness. You have an evident and secret ambition. You love distinctions, honors; the least of them puffs you up ridiculously. On the other hand, you believe yourself called to perfection; and there is not a religious congregation who would wish to keep you after a three-months' novitiate. You have been flattered for a long time; you are no longer flattered here — it is that which you cannot endure. I repeat, take care! there is in all this great danger. Sometimes you would wish to act better, to avoid real evil, to do real good; but there is in you a principle which stifles everything, and unceasingly gains ground; when it will have gained all, invaded all, you will be ruined; and already, under very austere, very ecclesiastical appearances, there is almost nothing priestly in your soul. You have scarcely either any charity or real zeal; charity and zeal are visibly becoming extinguished in your heart; you have hardly ever a thought for the spiritual advancement of your children. Once more, take care! *Vastitas et sterilitas;* behold that with which the Scripture threatens the proud, 'You are devoured by pride, and necessarily will be sterile.' Again the Scripture says, *Sicut lignum aridum in deserto.* Do you wish that I should give you a trait of your character which will aid you to know yourself? You admire nothing, you never praise any one; that is decisive. You will, I fear, end badly; or rather, no; your desire and the grace of God will save you, and you will end well."

He has really ended well; he has become a generous and devoted priest. What happiness to meet with sincere and courageous souls, that do not rebel against truth respecting themselves, and who, once enlightened, generously put their hands to the work!

CHAPTER XIV.

SECOND SOURCE OF DEFECTS IN MAN AND IN THE CHILD: SENSUALITY.

THERE is, besides pride, another deep wound of the human heart, another generating source of defects and vices without number in man and in the child; it is sensuality, that is to say, the inordinate desire for the pleasures of the senses. St. John calls it *concupiscentia carnis;* St. Paul, effeminacy: *Neque molles*, says he; and it is actually nothing else but an unworthy and cowardly effeminacy of the mind, the heart, and the senses. We ought to make here, from the point of view regarding education, a particular study of it, because it is for education a danger to be feared, and the source of the most painful difficulties. We shall first speak of the origin and disorder of it; then of the fatal sway it exercises over human life, especially over children and young people; and, in fine, we shall seek out what resources education prepares to combat it, and what are the remedies possible for opposing it.

I.

If we wish to understand properly what this disastrous wound of human nature is, and the particular difficulties it creates for education, it is necessary to go back to the chief source of all evil, even to the original fall. "God made man upright," says the philosopher; "and this uprightness," as Bossuet explains, "consists in the mind being perfectly submissive to God, the body likewise being perfectly submissive to the mind. But the revolt of the spirit against God led to the revolt of the flesh against the spirit." And again Bossuet says, "Since original sin, the passions of the flesh, by a just punishment of God, have become tyrannical; man has been plunged in the pleasures of the senses; and, according to the words of St. Augustine, instead of being, as he ought to be, through his primitive immortality and the perfect submission of the body to the mind, spiritual even in the flesh, he has become carnal in mind." Through original sin the primitive equilibrium has been broken, and the sad result of this rupture has been a frightful predominance of the body over the soul. Hence in us a strong desire for sensuous pleasures, and an irregularity, the disorder of which is something more humiliating and more vile even than pride. Pride is a usurpation, a criminal madness, but in which still sparkles a trace, a remembrance, of dignity; it is the mind of man being honored by itself, and being exalted at the expense of truth and justice. Sensuality has nothing in it but vileness; it is the most miserable of the captivities of the soul; it is the mind becoming subject to the flesh. The sensual man has no other end, no other God but his body: *Quorum Deus venter est*, St. Paul energetically says. Who does not feel that there is here a deplorable forfeiture, a frightful degradation, and the overthrow of all the nobility of human life, in this insult given to the nature and dignity of man? Man is the king of creation. But how — through his senses, through his body? Certainly not; in this relation, there are animals who vie with him. There are some of them, who, in certain respects, prevail over him; who are more agile and stronger than he. There are some who do what he could never do; who wander over the bosom of the waters, who hover in the immense spaces of the air. Man is the king of creation through his mind, through his intelligence, through his soul. It is through his soul he is reasonable, through his soul he is free, through his soul he is immortal, through his soul that he has sway over all nature. That which should reign in man, that which should govern his life, is, therefore, his soul.

The body is but a slave, and should only obey. Nevertheless, what does sensuality? It reverses this divine order; it causes the body to predominate over the soul; it enslaves the soul to the senses. The body has its instincts, its appetites; sensual, earthly, carnal, impetuous, blind, regarding neither reason, nor faith, nor honor. The soul has its tastes and its wants, its aspirations and its tendencies; noble, elevated, pure, wise, reasonable, accepting rule and bridle. But the sensual inclinations oppress the aspirations of the soul. For this reason there is a struggle, a necessary struggle, eternally between these two powers so opposed. It is necessary to choose, — whether the senses shall be repressed, governed, subjected to reason, to faith, to honor, and, the soul being mistress, life shall be maintained in its dignity; or whether the senses shall rule, shall enslave the soul, and life become debased.

Alas! I speak of struggles; and how many men are there who no longer strive, who abdicate, who wantonly deliver themselves up to this debasement of their life, this shameful servitude of the soul! Certainly the evil is profound; it lies even in the bowels of human nature. It is universal; sensuality, in one way or other, causes every one to feel its pricks. It is this degrading yoke, as the Scripture says, which weighs on all the children of Adam, from the day they came from the womb of their mother till the day they re-enter the bosom of their common mother, the earth. It is the most terrible result and most manifest token of this original forfeiture, by which the human creature, who wished to elevate himself to the height of God, fell even below his own nature, and paid by the most grievous humiliations the madness of his pride. I know well that childhood is not the age in which this inclination breaks out in its full force; nevertheless the evil lies deep in the child himself, and it is often to be found there exercising a dreadful sway. At this age everything favors sensuality. I speak not only of these sad hereditary seeds in the souls of all the children of Adam; I speak of the predominance of the physical life over the intellectual and moral life; I speak of the development of the senses which comes before that of reason; and in fine, if all must be said, of the senseless manner in which the greater number of parents bring up, in this respect, their very young children. I ought to dwell on this point, which has results for ultimate education that the greater number of parents, in their blind tenderness, do not seem even to suspect, but which are not less fatal. I ought to point out this danger, too much despised and too common. Do they comprehend, do they appear to comprehend, the sad but too real truths which we are speaking of? Do they dream of the presence of this dreaded enemy called sensuality in the souls of children, and of the extreme danger there is in developing this unfortunate inclination in childhood, and furnishing it with its stings? There is really room to doubt it, when we see the care which the greater number of parents take to cultivate and humor it in every way in their children. What do fathers, and especially mothers, think of — I do not say in the newly-born child, but in the child who already begins to understand matters, and whose dawning intellect is capable of culture and advancement — for example, in the child of four or five years old? What is it they give most care to in this child — what is it they nourish in him — what is it they develop in him? Is it the reasonable creature? is it the mind, the heart, the soul? No; it is the material creature; the body, the animal life. Yes; there are thousands of poor little children brought up in this manner: overwhelmed with physical cares; saturated with dainties; their little faces, their little persons, idolized; all the most foolish, and sometimes the most ridiculous, fripperies sought for, to clothe them; they are adorned, as it were, for public exhibition, then they are flattered, they are incensed, they are adored. This excites pity, and is an evil to see. Let no one speak here to me of necessity, or of health; necessity has a measure — the senseless mania that I denounce knows it not, and health itself suffers from these pitiful cares. But it is especially the souls of these unfortunate children that suffer from this; the physical development stifles not only that of the mind, but vanity, thus excited, germinates, and takes total possession of these poor intoxicated little heads; effeminacy establishes its empire in them, enervates, numbs, paralyzes them; inspires them with an inexpressible indolence, a horror of effort and labor, which destroys all their energy, all their activity, and prepares for their future education the most serious difficulties. I confine myself to pointing out here the two principal of them, — sloth, and injury to morals.

II.

I say that sensuality, especially when favored by an effeminate education, inevitably engenders in children a deplorable slothfulness. It may be asked, are not all children idle? Without doubt they are, and who does not know it? But it is necessary to know also that there are two kinds of idleness. There is the idleness which has its origin in the thoughtlessness of the age; that is not the most dangerous, and in the end we succeed in curing it; it is necessary to wait, without trifling with it, till the character, the mind, the reason, and the body itself, attain a certain development. The love of labor, especially mental labor, cannot spring up immediately. Childhood, naturally lively, uncertain, and eager, can keep still neither its body nor its tongue; it talks, laughs, and continually jumps about, without reflection or system; it prefers play to serious matters. That will pass away. Much patience, and also much encouragement, is necessary with such children—something which excites and takes hold of them; much persistency, with a firmness always benevolent, and sometimes indulgent: in a word, never to permit the child to become indolent, or to get the better of you; but also neither to crush nor dishearten him. I can scarcely recollect having ever despaired of a child idle through thoughtlessness and giddiness, or have sent away such children. When we know how to win them, we bring it to an end sooner or later, and oftentimes very soon. But there is another idleness,—the inertness which arises from a weak nature, without energy or elasticity; this idleness is almost incurable, at least unless one applies himself to its cure in very good time by well-contrived means equally mild and firm. But an early education, such as that which I depicted just now, is one of the greatest obstacles such a cure can meet with. The cares, efforts, and perseverance that will be required later on to save a child thus brought up, in order to make a worker of him, to make a man of him, are incredible. And how many times do they fail! Let parents take care, then, and not create beforehand terrible and almost unsurmountable difficulties for the education of their children. One fails so much the more, because this intellectual and physical effeminacy is usually accompanied by effeminacy of the heart, a sort of moral apathy, and insensibility. Now, Fénelon has rightly said of it, "Of all the troubles of education, none is to be compared with that of bringing up children deficient in sensibility. Quick, feeling natures may fall into terrible disorders; the passions and presumption may hurry them away; but they have also great resources, and can be reclaimed, though far gone — instruction is in them a hidden germ which puts forth shoots and bears fruit when experience comes to the aid of reason, and the passions cool; at least, we know by what means we can render them attentive and arouse their curiosity. They have in them a something which causes them to become interested in what is taught to them, and their honor may be piqued; instead of which we have no hold on indolent natures. All the thoughts of the latter are distractions; they are never where they ought to be; even correction cannot sting them to the quick; they hear all, and feel nothing. This indolence renders the child negligent and disgusted with everything he does; the best education, then, runs the risk of shipwreck, if we do not hasten to get before the evil during the earliest years of childhood." Is it this that effeminate education, unfortunately so general in the present day, does for young children? Thanks be to God, when it does not prepare another danger still more to be feared: I speak of the danger to their morals.

III.

I border here on a subject particularly delicate and painful; I touch one of the greatest wounds of man and the child, also one of the most terrible rocks in the way of education. I shall have some severe words to say — without doubt, I shall surprise more than one mother, ignorant of the perils around her dear child, and perhaps confiding too much in an innocence, which, during a long time, has not existed. But, since I am led to treat here of such a subject, I must have the courage to speak the necessary truths, and to tell them to all those who have need of hearing them — to children, to masters, to parents themselves. Ah! if there be anything beautiful, amiable, heavenly, on earth, it is innocence in a young man, in a child; a heart, a soul, which evil has not yet approached, which is ignorant of it, or has been preserved from its stains; an innocent, candid, virginal soul, which has retained all its freshness, all its bloom, all its perfume. Who can describe the grace, the charm, the nobility, the dignity, the honor, of it! It is sweet to meet with such a soul on earth — to contemplate, to love it. We recognize in it without trouble, we are sensible of, an indescribable sign of happiness, some reflection of itself on a mild and pure physiognomy. We are charmed at seeing all the early limpidity of this countenance, all the innocent candor of this mien, and this amiable face. This soul has not only all its grace, but it has still its first sap, its ardor, its vigor, its power; as it were, nothing in it has been defiled, nothing has been exhausted; life flows on in its primitive abundance — it keeps its faculties, with all their treasures, their wealth of energy, intact; with its grace and strength it retains all its tenderness. Vice, which might have defiled it, cooled or extinguished its flame, having never breathed over it, that pure flame, that flame of good and holy affections, lighted up by God himself, has been preserved there as in a sanctuary. We know that a man, too celebrated for his unbelief and scandals, has, in a moment of sincerity and frankness, uttered this very true speech: "I maintain, a young man who has retained his innocence up to twenty years of age, is, at that age, the most generous, the best, the most amiable, of men." Such is innocence in a child, in a young man — more charming, more touching, perhaps, in this happy age, which is ignorant of everything, and in which strife against innocence has not yet come to disturb it; though more worthy of respect, and in some manner more sacred in a heart which already feels its place disputed, but which guards it, and in which it then becomes virtue. But what a holy and dreadful charge for a father, for a mother, for masters, to guard this soul, this heart, during childhood and through youth, even to mature age; to lead it to the age of manhood through all the perils of ignorance and temptation, without permitting this purity, this beauty, this charm, to be blighted; without permitting this crown to be lost! What a work! what incomparable happiness! and also what invaluable service! It must be admitted with a sigh, that it is rare, and it is here we may well cry out, in sight of such universal shipwrecks, *apparent rari.* We live in an evil age, where innocence is vainly sought for; we scarcely longer meet among us those countenances full of candor, in which the sweet attractions of this amiable virtue shine. Innocence! innocence! childhood itself is no longer acquainted with you — it blushes for you. This age has lost its artless charm, since frightful corruption seems to sit by its cradle in order to watch its awakening. The child of our days appears ripened before his time by vice — precocious and damaged fruit, which libertinism gathers during the morning of life, and, without trouble, detaches from virtue; soon becoming a prey to all the ravages of vice, it disappears in the bloom of life, leaving behind an odor of death. Here is what too frequently becomes of youth, and even of childhood, among us. But let us hasten to say, also — and let it be sufficient consolation and encouragement for those whose sacred duty it is to bring up and save children for God — all do not perish in this shipwreck. No; whatever may be the weaknesses of this age, and the wretchedness of the corrupted times in which we live, we can never be justified in believing that childhood is fatally cast, as it were, into a pasture of vice, while there are happy examples of young people retaining their chaste innocence to the epoch of priestly education, or even, in the world, to the hour of a blessed marriage, bearing witness that parents and the religious teachers of youth have at their disposal efficacious means for saving this age, so tender and so exposed. Yes, there are still among us, thanks to Heaven, virtuous, Christian families, profoundly blessed by God, in which piety and good morals are cultivated. Noble traditions, great examples, simple and strong virtues, form there, as it were, an atmosphere of honor and purity, which the child inhales from his birth, amid which he happily grows up, which creates for him a healthy and pure temperament, and which gives him, with the instinctive horror of evil, holy habits of modesty, decency, and respect. There are houses of education, where so strict a guard is placed around the youth whose innocence they shelter, that evil is averted, and under the eyes of God, and the wings of religion, virtue is preserved and strengthened for the strife of the future. I have had the consolation of living in a house, of which a religious, one of the holiest and most clear-sighted — the Père de Ravignan — could say to me after a retreat, "I do not know if there be in the world a house where there can be more innocence than in yours." I recall to mind with emotion one day — it was Easter Monday — when a man of great intellect, great experience, a celebrated laureate of the University, a Christian, and otherwise very virtuous, dining with us at Gentilly, under our trees, already verdant and in blossom, and seeing the pure joy of these children, the candor of their countenances, the innocence of their frolics and their shouts, said suddenly, turning towards me, "What happiness to think that perhaps there is not one of these children who may not be pure and in favor with God!" [1] Yes, childhood can be saved, and, if it be lost, it is frequently because it has not been suffi-

[1] He was, nevertheless, a very original and very amusing man; very strong in Latin verse. Some moments after, as the children were singing a hymn according to their fashion in honor of the Holy Virgin, he suddenly cried out, "Ah, there is a mortal sin!" It was a false verse.

ciently watched over, either at college, or even sometimes, it must be said, at the domestic hearth. There is here a terrible responsibility and a very grave subject for the meditation of parents and those who fill their place, for the ravages of evil are frequently frightful. It is enough to cause a shudder! Yes, when vice has taken hold of a poor child, a poor young man, it is impossible to describe what it makes of him, whither it drives him. When this evil becomes contagious, and, like the plague, gradually spreads in a house of education, or any other, it is terrible to see the victims it strikes, the ruins it heaps up. Mothers! mothers of families! watch, watch over your children in your houses, at your sides; for there, even there, close by you, and, so to say, under the shadow of your wings, the evil may seize and devour them. There are perils close by you, around you, among you. Professors, directors, superiors, open your eyes; be vigilant; behold the enemy, the dreaded enemy; if he penetrate, if he enter, he will devastate your house, he will ruin all; he will cast victim upon victim, dead upon dead! Nevertheless, when this evil has possession of a young heart, its sad and lugubrious symptoms may be quickly perceived. What sudden change has been wrought in this child? He was merry, frank, loving; behold him suddenly sad, restless, gloomy, defiant, dissimulating. He has no longer his candid smile, his blooming countenance, his open heart, his expansive soul; something has passed over his physiognomy, and has cast, as it were, a veil on it; something is there, in that heart, which contracts it;

something he does not wish to show, like a shameful secret that he hides. The poor child! whither is a first step about to conduct him? At first he hesitated, he blushed, he trembled; soon he no longer hesitates, he no longer blushes, he no longer trembles. One fall leads to another; one abyss decoys to another; weakness increases, habit becomes formed — terrible habit, which triumphs over will, reason, honor, faith, conscience, everything. He no longer hears anything, he no longer sees anything; it becomes a frenzy. Insensibility, impudence, get the better of him. He inflicts outrage upon outrage, ignominy upon ignominy. Who will stop him in his disorders? Who will recover him from such a weakness? Who will break off such habits? Who will burst such bonds? Alas! who does not know that there is nothing, nothing in the world, so difficult to correct in a child as secret habits of impurity? And whither will they conduct him? What is to become of him? What will become of his education, his future, his life? Vice will soon have blighted, killed, everything in him — his body first — his health receives a mortal taint. Poor child, scarcely beginning life, he has exhausted and dried up its sources. This frail organization, which has not yet acquired its development, its consistency, its strength, he abuses in every way; he undermines, he corrupts, he destroys it. Nature cannot be outraged with impunity — outraged nature revenges itself, and its vengeance is terrible; sometimes slow, it always comes. The fresh coloring of that young face has already disappeared, and given place to an accusing paleness; his eyes have become extinguished; precocious lines already furrow his forehead; his whole constitution wears out and decays — life goes on, death arrives — an old man at twenty years of age; see him verging towards his grave, where, as the Scripture says, "his vices shall descend with him, and dishonor his ashes." Behold the fruits of vice for so many unfortunate children and young people! — a premature death, or at least a debilitated life; the health impaired for ever. The ruins of mind and heart are not less great. In these shameful habits the mind loses its elasticity and its vigor, its delicacy and its grace; enervated by vile enjoyment, plunged in the mire of the senses, it becomes blunted, it becomes numbed, it wallows in sloth and torpor. The imagination, possessed by a settled idea which it pursues, tormented by impure phantoms, can no longer turn away from them; it has neither intellectual vigor nor moral power; the exercise of thought only wearies; love of good finds there a surfeited heart, when it does not find it hardened; the sensual child no longer labors, no longer studies, no longer loves. He no longer loves: sensual vice profoundly impairs the character, and kills the heart in those who gives themselves up to it. The child was born good, sweet and amiable, simple and sincere; he had a candor of soul, and a mild serenity of temper, arising from the peace of a pure conscience; but, since the fatal habits of vice have invaded him, that equality, which had its source in the calmness of the soul, is no more than a peevish, capricious, whimsical temper; that candor, which displayed his whole soul, shows but gloomy and hidden thoughts. He has lost, with his innocence, that which constituted his greatest charm. In like manner, the source of the best and purest affections has been dried up in that worn-out heart. It has been remarked, that corrupted children are incapable of gratitude, and have not any elevated or generous feeling. The habit of egotistical enjoyment interdicts disinterested pleasures; and the most withering reproach has been inflicted as a chastisement by the writer whom I indicated just now as rendering an unsuspected homage to virtue: "I have always seen," says Rousseau, "that children corrupted at an early age become wicked and cruel. They know neither pity nor mercy. They will sacrifice father, mother, and the entire universe, to the least of their pleasures." To enjoy is everything for them; the rest is nothing. Nevertheless, sensual children sometimes have the air of having a good heart; but it is necessary not to be deceived by it—it is a false appearance. The appearance of sensibility in children should be studied with great care by masters; it is in the highest degree important to look well into the source of it, and see if it come from the heart, or the senses: if it come from the heart, it is good, valuable, and a great resource for the education of the child; but, if it come from the senses and the evil tenderness of an effeminate heart, it is false and very dangerous. There must be no doubt on this point. Nothing is more egotistical and harder than a corrupted child, whatever appearances he may have. That caressing tenderness which he sometimes evinces, and which resembles the blossom of affection, has sad roots, an evil nature; if we look closely into it, we shall not be slow to see that this flower is mud. It is necessary to be kind to such children, but rarely tender, except with great gravity; they must never be permitted, but with extreme reserve, sensible manifestations of their effeminate tenderness; for example, never to embrace them, or allow one's self to be embraced by them. They require much compassion, but it should be firm and dignified. These children resemble damaged fruit: look at an apple — while we do not see that there is a worm in its heart, it seems sound and good; let us open it, we find there but rottenness. But this is enough on these sad subjects. It is enough to make whosoever is charged with bringing up childhood understand the fears and all the vigilance necessary on this point. Let us now see how we can prevent and combat so great an evil.

CHAPTER XV.

WHAT IS TO BE DONE IN ORDER TO SAVE CHILDREN FROM THE DANGERS OF SENSUALITY.

It is to parents solely that I first address myself, for the care of preserving their children concerns them above all others. Among the duties of paternal and maternal authority, there is none more serious, more delicate, more sacred. Carelessness, even thoughtlessness, in this respect, would be, not alone unpardonable, but they cannot be imagined in parents — I do not say Christian — but those having simply the commonest tenderness for their children. If every honor confided by God to his creatures has a corresponding duty, so much the more serious as the honor is greater, what solicitude is there not imposed on those who have received from God the incomparable deposit of the soul of a child — the deposit of such weakness and such innocence! In order to express my idea, I will borrow from the Scriptures a simple and forcible expression: I will say that parents should watch over their children as over the apple of their eye. But do they always sufficiently understand in practice all that is comprised in this high and holy obligation, and even to what point solicitude and prudence must be carried? May they not be, and are they not, too frequently, culpably ignorant and deplorably deluded on this subject? I will say at once, it is at a very early age, from the first years, and, if I may say so, from the cradle, that it is necessary to think of preserving soul and body from effeminacy and its frightful results, to lay the foundation of good morals in children by a strict education and the extreme of vigilance. But what means must they use, and to what precautions must they have recourse? Some details are required here. On account of the gravity and sanctity of the subject, I may be excused those into which I am going to enter. I will simply give my idea on each matter relating to it. It is of supreme importance to accustom children to modesty, to decency, in every thing respecting themselves; to inspire them with a great bashfulness. In order to arrive at this, it is necessary to watch well over their going to rest, their sleeping, and their rising; to take care to cover them well; especially never to allow them to sleep together, nor with other persons; to abstain from all familiarity with regard to them — nevertheless, without affectation; to watch their plays; to make them avoid all unsuitable behavior among themselves; never to permit them any kind of rude, indecent liberties, as is sometimes done under pretext of amusing tricks. On all these matters, children must be given, from the earliest age, elevated and pure precedents. It is strictly necessary never to permit ourselves the most trifling liberty whatsoever before them. The ancient maxim should always be under the eye of every family, especially every Christian family, *Maxima debetur puero reverentia: si quid turpe paras, ne tu pueri contempseris annos.* Woe to the parents of whom Tacitus has said, "It is sometimes the parents themselves who habituate their children to licentiousness and vice, instead of honor and virtue" — *Quandoque etiam ipsi parentes nec probitati neque modestiæ parvulos assuefaciunt, sed lasciviæ et libertati.* (Dial. de Orator. 29.) And (Quintilian, book i. c. 4), *Nos docuimus, ex nobis audierunt,* etc. — "It is we ourselves who have instructed them in evil; it is from us they have learned it!" Let them always remember, then, to watch with strict attention every word they utter at the domestic fireside: children always listen, and understand more than they suppose; and a single word may do them mortal injury. Carefully remove from their sight every dangerous object, — bad books, bad pamphlets, bad newspapers, whether illustrated or not, or bad pictures. This is the gravest, the strictest duty. What is to be said of the negligence of certain parents in this respect, and of everything that is to be seen exhibited on the tables of certain drawing-rooms? I cannot resist citing here an incredible example of imprudence and laxity which I myself witnessed. A young man of fifteen years of age had received for his new-year's gift, magnificently bound, a complete collection of the works of a contemporary author, a poet and celebrated novelist, whose name I shall not mention. Every one knows he has written too much, and sometimes too freely, for his entire works to be placed with impunity in the hands of a young man. I one day entered the house of this child's parents, accompanied by a respectable magistrate. The boy was there with his books. "What are these beautiful volumes?" asked the magistrate. The mother, with some embarrassment, named the author. The magistrate could not prevent himself from evincing surprise. "But at least," replied he, "I hope this young man will not read these ——, nor these ——." "He has already read them," answered the boy. I went out on the moment, in order to relieve the mother from the visible restraint my presence had placed upon her. Imprudent mother! how had she understood her duty! And the volumes had been sent by a near relative!

Another point which again requires the greatest vigilance from parents is that of servants, children's maids, valets, coachmen, grooms; I will go further, and, at the risk of surprising not a few, I will say even nurses. How many times have we not said that parents do not sufficiently understand all the injury their grievous negligence, their too much blind confidence, in this respect, may cause to children! One day, a mother, driven to despair by having her son sent away from an educational establishment for a shameful fault, in a transport of passion said to the superior, "If my son is acquainted with evil, sir, it is in your house he has learned it; he was pure when I confided him to you!" But the superior, being unfortunately better informed, replied to her, "No, madam, it is not here your son has learned evil. You have in your house, at the present moment, a domestic who has all your confidence; it is he who has ruined your son. Interrogate your child yourself." These people, even though they may not be, as is too often seen, known corrupters, are so coarse in their education, their manners, and their language, that children left to them can easily learn many evil things, if they be not well and closely watched. It is necessary to be not less careful respecting the companions who visit them: children learn evil from one another, and it is in this way they usually go wrong. Every mother must know, that, owing to the unhappy times we live in, every little companion may be dangerous for her child; and it is there she must begin to exercise her watchfulness. The greater number of children, especially in towns, have, from the earliest age, lost their innocence in different degrees. Not one who may not have drunk more or less poison! not one who does not know at least something, if not everything, of evil! not one among the sons of Adam who may not have instincts, sensual tastes, extremely to be dreaded, with respect to purity! not one, who, if he be not rigorously watched over, may not be capable of those liberties, those improper familiarities, which can so quickly lead to everything bad! Children who are permitted to visit freely are always a danger to each other. As I write for the instruction of every one, parents as well as masters, I ought to speak of everything, and not shrink from any useful detail. I will then say, Keep your eyes open with fear and vigilance, not only on the little companions who visit your children, but likewise on male and female cousins, among whom familiarities are frequently but the more dangerous, on account of being more easily carried on. I go further, and not without reason: watch over even brothers and sisters. Yes, when there are many children in a family, who put on or take off their clothing in the same room before one another, and who may often find themselves alone together, there is a danger for both which demands all the vigilance of parents. Why should I be obliged to speak of these matters? and will parents believe me? I shall have at least performed my duty by telling them: it is frequently under their roof, and almost under their eyes — closed by an unhappy and false security — that evil befalls their children; and how can they prevent it? They do not even suspect it. All this is grievous to speak of; but it is the truth. Yes; in spite of the presumed innocence of their age, children, whatsoever they may be, must be distrusted, and have a watchful eye over them in everything. I will plainly ask parents — blind, weak, as they are, regarding the most evident defects, the least pardonable faults, of their sons and their daughters — do they sincerely, freely, wish for the preservation of their innocence? or do they at least attach to this great and supreme matter all the importance that it deserves? There is certainly room to doubt of it. They excuse, they color, they find reasons for, everything in children. For instance, a child shows too lively an inclination for pleasure; the mother tells you, "Oh! there is no room for anxiety; it is not what one imagines; it is all simply an open-hearted and undisguised nature." But he betrays himself by an obscene word; it is purely a sally of playful humor; he has never seen anything wrong. And they thus answer everything; excuse everything. I declare, I have frequently found the children less insupportable by their vices than the parents by their whims. I have but one question to put here to those unfortunate parents: Do you, or do you not, wish your children to be innocent? Well, use the means then — all the means — necessary for it. Nothing is superfluous. But no; I fear you do not wish it. There is, however, at least one thing you wish: you desire health, renown, fortune, long life, for them, and affection for yourself. You desire at least all that. Well, blind as you are, know that it is but on condition of being virtuous that these things are to be secured. If you desire these, wish for what gives them; do not be inconsistent. But no; you do not seriously desire even that; you give everything up to chance. If you seriously desired it, would you cast these poor children — for how can I forget this danger? — would you cast them into these public schools, I ought to say these gulfs, that we know of? I do not attack, I do not name, any of them; in fine, we know that authoritative voices, from all parts, have been loudly raised against them. There are such houses where a child is certainly ruined if he enter; and you place him there! Well, I maintain, myself, that parents cannot conscientiously, for any reason, or on any account, place their children in such houses. They will say, What are we to do? Everything except what you do. Though you may have much to say, and much to allege, God will not excuse you. You will not have done what you ought, what you could have done, for your child. It may be you do not place him in one of these houses of perdition; you keep him at home; you give him a tutor. But you will choose this tutor among a thousand — observe what I say — among a thousand? In fine, suppose the tutor excellent; do you believe, that, in providing him, all is done, and that your child can no longer need other assistance? To confine myself to one of the most important needs, do you think that his piety can be sustained in such a manner as to preserve his heart from all dangerous impressions within and without, from all the snares that surround — even in the best-watched houses — the innocence of a poor child, if you do not give this new-born and weak piety the necessary support of sound instruction and the sacraments? Ere long, there are indications, alas! too certain, which cause you anxiety. You come to seek us, to confide to us your anxieties, your vexations; your tears, to ask our advice: but will you follow this advice? We can never prevail upon you to do that; necessarilly, we propose in such a case the indispensable aid of regular, frequent confession. Oh! but that cannot be; there would be such a master to be inconvenienced, such a lesson to be lost. You do not wish it; and, nevertheless, you wish your son to be saved: you wish an impossibility. I will then say to those mothers who require to hear it, You believe our word to be more efficacious than it is; you send your children to us once, twice, at rare and long intervals; what do you wish us to do? Can such habits be cured, even in persons of mature age, much less in children, except by very frequent confession? Nevertheless, you become re-assured; you congratulate yourselves: "Oh! my son confesses to Father So-and-so, who is a saint." Well, as for me, I tell you, that, with your method of directing your children, even a saint could do nothing for them. If you wish that, this saint should do anything, send your child to him frequently and regularly, and induce the child to perform with docility all that his confessor desires him. Pardon this warmth of language; I am drawn into it by the ever-recurring remembrance of what I have seen caused by the blindness and inconsistency of certain parents on this very serious point. No; I cannot express as forcibly as I wish how much constant, attentive, steady solicitude is required in everything on the part of parents, in order to preserve their young children from the evil that surrounds and attacks them on all sides. I recapitulate. It is during the tenderest age that it is necessary to be warmly solicitous and watchful over a young child; it is then that precaution should be carried into the most trifling details: the manner of putting on his clothes; the care of removing from him everything not strictly conformable to modesty; to be careful in inspiring habits of decency and respect; at the same time, to keep from his sight and hearing everything that may be perilous; to banish from the domestic fireside every loose word, every book, every scandalous object; in fine, to watch over everything that surrounds him — and every one who approaches him — servants, companions, relatives, even brothers and sisters: all these cares are necessary in order to save children, and present them pure and innocent, to the masters whose office it will be to continue the home education. And at last, when they must be confided to a college or a master, be strict — very strict — in the choice, and never relax in vigilance.

CHAPTER XVI.

CURIOSITY; LEVITY; THIRD SOURCE OF DEFECTS IN MAN AND IN THE CHILD.

PRIDE and sensuality are terrible vices, that must be attacked boldly, and forcibly subdued. When a soul is capable of this struggle, however profoundly enrooted these vices may be, nothing is to be despaired of; and, the efforts of the teacher meeting with a happy concurrence in the soul of him whom he brings up, the work of education is still possible. But what strongly compromises it, what brings to it, I will almost say, the most hopeless of obstacles, what too frequently renders the most devoted cares, the most skilful masters, unavailing, is a third and unhappy defect, which causes everything to glide over the child, and does not permit anything to penetrate into his soul. I speak of levity, daughter of that deadly vice which the apostle names concupiscence of the eyes, *concupiscentia oculorum.* Concupiscence of the eyes is to be met with in the child, in the young man, as well as the grown man, but under a particular form. In the child it is fickleness, heedlessness, giddy curiostiy. Now, the fickle, heedless, inquisitive soul, open on all sides, allows everything to be lost, and keeps nothing; no serious work is possible with it or in it. I have had to struggle very particularly against this defect. I know all the difficulties it brings into education; I have been obliged to combat it, at one and the same time, in the children and in the masters. I had, one year, in one of the seminaries that I directed, among some excellent masters, many young professors, good, but too young in age and character, heedless on their own account, and also on account of the children; thoughtless in mind and heart, and who did not sufficiently understand the gravity of their mission, or all the importance of their duties. I had also some children of the same stamp, who never looked seriously on anything in their education or their life. For a time I feared that the spirit of levity was being introduced into the house, and then all the rest was hopeless. I ought to dwell on this capital defect, and hold on this subject, addressing all who require to hear me many conversations, in which I shall apply myself to make all the miseries and dangers of levity comprehensible. It is, indeed, very important that children should know it well. This defect, the most usual at their age, and also too frequently the most excused, is not the less a fatal defect, and may, if it be persisted in, if it be not combated, ruin not only childhood, but the whole life. It is more than necessary that men charged with so grave a work as education should understand all the gravity and seriousness it requires on their part, and how incompatible levity of mind and disposition is with it. In fine, I will add, that parents also must be very sensible of all the mature reflection that the dignity of father and mother claims from those who bear it, and that it cannot rest securely on thoughtless heads.

I.

I say, then, there is in the child a kind of eager, restless curiosity, opening his eyes and his desires to everything, and which is exactly characterized by the name of *concupiscentia oculorum.* It is the opening of the eyes and the soul to everything outside that attracts and seduces it; it is all the thoughtless, indiscreet, unrestrained inclination of seeing everything; it is an unbridled curiosity for evil as well as good, a passionate cupidity; hence it is that love of pleasure degenerates into this vice. Moralists also say, with reason, that the concupiscence of the eyes touches closely on concupiscence of the flesh. Who has not observed, even among the most innocent children, that love of amusement and pleasure is usually very lively — the wish to see everything, to hear everything, to feel everything? This love of pleasure, of enjoyment, betrays itself at first by the love of play, the passion for amusement, which sometimes becomes a frenzy in them. It is an early and real danger, and must be watched. But what is most to be feared is the pleasure of the eyes, or the desire of seeing everything; the pleasure of the ears, or the desire of hearing everything; the pleasure of the taste, or the desire of tasting everything. It is very dangerous for a child, or a young man, to allow his soul to be thus not only accessible to every seduction, but passionately tending towards them. At a certain age, especially when man begins to be initiated into the secrets of life, the love of visible objects may, if the young man do not watch over himself with strict attention, cause a thousand tyrants, vile as they are imperious, to penetrate him. From that time he will have lost all dominion over himself; he will be dispossessed of his soul, and drawn into a whirlwind of illusions, whose plaything he will unceasingly be, until, after the most grievous mistakes, after virtue, duty, labor, career, have all been sacrificed, he falls into a frightful void. This passionate cupidity, this eagerness for seeing everything, this taste, this habit of living and casting one's self abroad, usually engenders an unbounded restlessness, an everlasting dissipation, which hurries away the moments, the hours, the days, the whole life, of a young man. This love of pleasure, when it is not, as among young children, the need of motion, is, if it be not the source of vices, at least the door and entrance for them. Fénelon says, "It opens the soul like a dismantled fortress to all the attacks of the enemy." When this defect has not a real depth of good sense as a counterpoise, when it is not alone a weakness of age, which wears out with the increase of years, but an inherent vice in the nature, in the character, it is to be dreaded beyond measure. I know that this is not the idea always entertained of it; people are sometimes deceived, and very sadly so, with respect to it. As this defect appears to belong more to the age than to the child, as it is very frequently accompanied by amiable or brilliant qualities, they hope it will pass away; while waiting, they excuse it, and delude themselves as to its serious consequences. Certainly Fénelon did not take this view of it when he said that levity extinguished all piety, rendered one incapable of all serious application, and consumed every virtue. For my part, I know few vices more dangerous, and that require to be more seriously combated; when levity becomes persistent, it is one of the most terrible obstacles to education, and sometimes the ruin of an entire life. The truth is, there is nothing to be done for thoughtless beings, or by thoughtless beings. It is very proper that I should distinguish the trifling frivolities of early age from that fundamental and essential defect called *levity*. Levity, thus understood, is so grave an affair in my eyes, that, if it were permissible to assert that there are some children incapable of being brought up, I would say, without hesitation, they are heedless children. And how will you bring up such natures? All the labor of education, all the most skilled cares, are ruined beforehand by this unfortunate defect, which, as I have said, causes everything to glide over the surface, and does not allow anything to penetrate to the bottom. Why do I say to the bottom? — there is no bottom in them. A heedless soul is a soul open on all sides, and closed nowhere; the bottom is wanting. In vain you lavish on it the most elaborate teaching; it is a sieve; all passes through, and nothing remains in it. A heedless child retains nothing, can do nothing, hears nothing; what will you do with such a child? It is not thus with other defects. They may be attacked boldly, and conquered after a sharp struggle. Pride can be humbled, transformed, and even sometimes converted into energy for good. There is also a hold on sensuality — it may be combated; but a heedless, restless, fickle soul, is it not, so to say, unseizable? For this reason, levity is so much to be dreaded, and so terribly compromises, if it be neglected, if it be allowed to subsist, the work of education. By it, indeed, all correspondence of the child with your best cares becomes impossible, and all your efforts remain stricken with sterility. The lamentable results of this defect are, inattention, irreflection, inconstancy, giddiness, in everything. Who has not remarked what a prodigious point incongruity of behavior attains in the heedless child? We see him present a spectacle of the most surprising variability; the most sudden, the most unexpected, changes. One day good, the next day bad; now sensible, now relapsing into heedlessness; fervent one moment, lukewarm the next; in heaven to-day, perhaps in hell to-morrow.

There are certain epochs of the year when the atmosphere is unsettled and the weather variable; the wind changes twenty times a day; sunshine suddenly succeeds rain; then the clouds soon return: we know not what to say of this weather; the most experienced is at fault. Thus it is in a heedless child or man; we can never know an instant beforehand what he will be, or what he will do the moment after. Just now, he was possessed by a mad gayety; at present, behold him sad and gloomy to excess. What has happened to him? We know not what idea has crossed his mind, and there is a cloud over his countenance; the thunder will soon burst forth, with a torrent of rain; but this emotion will soon pass away — nothing is profound in a heedless soul; the instant after you will see him plunge into a madcap joy. A poor soul, given up to curiosity, to levity, is really like the waves of the sea, delivered up to every wind. It is easy to understand that nothing steady, nothing serious, is possible in such a soul. Not a germ of virtue, not a principle, can take root there; it is not only an unstable earth, a moving sand, it is the mobility of a shadow. Plant a tree in the sea; assuredly it will not strike root there, nor will it give you fruit. Fatal to study, fatal to virtue, fatal to the future; behold, imprudent parents or masters, this levity of childhood, which causes you no anxiety, and which, perhaps, you find even amiable, and worthy of every indulgence! You intend to make a heedless child study; but what progress will he make? He hears not, he reflects not; neither does he seize or retain anything; all your explanations, all your lessons, fall to the ground for him. And what progress will he make in virtue? Virtue is energy, is constancy; such a nature is incapable of effort, and especially of persevering effort. His virtue, if he has any, comes and goes by fits and starts. He may have some aims towards good, but he soon falls back into the restlessness and vulgarity of his habitual conduct. His good resolutions are not sustained; they vanish on the first occasion. Virtue dwells in the soul, in the depths of the child; but, according to the words of the Gospel, all is on the surface, nothing is deep-rooted, in a heedless child: *Non habet radicem, sed est temporaneus:* he has no root, everything is ephemeral in him. And, at the same time, the power of running to waste is frightful in heedless souls; how they can squander the gifts of God, graces, faculties, natural and supernatural means, is not possible to describe. It is to these sad natures that the words of St. Bernard most properly apply: "Vases full of flaws, which let everything escape"—*Pleni rimarum, undequaque difluimus.* What serious future can be prepared in this condition? and how sorrowful it is to see these poor children going on, with a smile on their lips, and I know not how much careless gayety in their hearts, to the ruin of their life, and perhaps of their eternal future! Ah! unfortunate young man, you laugh, you jest, unceasingly; you thus abuse the most useful talents, losing every day the most valuable time of your every-day life in frivolities, in nonsense, when it is not in errors. Nevertheless, your education is not progressing, your defects become strengthened, your virtues lost, your piety extinguished; graces dry up, time flows on, the kingdom of God escapes you: where are you going? Nevertheless, God had designs for you. Perhaps He had given you a high vocation; what has become of it? Ah! you laugh; as for me, I weep—I weep over the abuse of gifts from God, over the waste of graces, over the sorrowful lowering of your soul and your life. I weep over a lost man. Yes, you might have become a man, a laborer for God in society or in the church, and you will never be but a silly, vulgar being, of a fruitless and barren mediocrity. Ah! you will make God and yourself bankrupt. Is there a greater misfortune in the world?

II.

The great evil to young people is in not being sufficiently brought into contact with mature age; in not considering sufficiently that they ought one day to be men, and that the man will have to suffer a long time, perhaps always, for the faults of the child. The great injury done by parents and masters is in not sufficiently pointing out the future seriousness of life, its labors, its duties, its dangers. They foolishly say, "Levity lasts but for a time; it passes away; it is only a matter of patience; let us wait." That is a great error. Without doubt, levity is especially a defect of childhood; setting aside the results of it, it may be corrected, and age will much assist; but age alone will not correct it. Levity, when one does not begin seriously with it, becomes strengthened by habit, changed into a second nature, clings to one through life, and is never to be got rid of. A heedless child, if he be not corrected in childhood, becomes a fickle man, still more incorrigible, and nothing can be more disastrous. For what is he but a fickle man? Is he brought up a man? is he even a man? does he deserve to get that name? Perhaps he is a magistrate, a priest, the father of a family: but if he be the plaything of inconstancy and perpetual restlessness; if he never lay himself down to anything, and unceasingly change; if he never resemble himself; if he never be on the morrow what he was the day before — what do I say, if he vary from hour to hour, from moment to moment, who can count on him, for an instant, in anything? Well, there are some men who are thus all their life, because they were left so in childhood; inattentive, thoughtless, whimsical, restless, without steadiness or consistency; like the leaf swept away by the wind, like wave driven by wave, or the bird borne on by the caprice of his wing. I ask, are these men? and if levity, which, after having ruined education and childhood, may ruin the whole life, is a matter to be neglected? or, rather, is it not during the entire life one of the most menacing dangers? In fine, what is such a life? who governs it? is it the fickle man who governs his life? No; he is governed from the outside by circumstances, by the thousand incidents of each hour; or, rather, he is not governed; he is pushed, tossed about by chance: once more, such a man is a plaything, the inconsistent and fragile plaything of every one and everything; he has been compared, and not without reason, to a dancing-jack, which acts at will by he knows not what thread moved by a strange hand. What dignity, what honor, can rest on him? Where is his gravity, his earnestness, his capacity, his firmness — where are his anchors, or his helm? What foundation can be made on such a man? To count on him, to found anything on him, is to count on the wind, to build on water or sand; to count himself as some one, to expect of him reflection, foresight, results of energy or will, any perseverance whatsoever, would be to take him for a man, and he is, alas! but a child. The Holy Scripture speaks somewhere of the child of a hundred years, *Puer centum annorum.* Well, yes, there are some men, who, even in mature age, even with gray hairs, have not yet come out of childhood, who are always children, on account of the levity, the thoughtlessness, the restlessness, the caprice, the weakness, and the inconsistency, of their character, *Puer centum annorum.* The Scripture adds a terrible word, *Puer centum annorum* PERIBIT —"The child of a hundred years shall perish!" Yes, he shall perish; the perils to which levity of disposition exposes him are frightful and numberless; perils for the honor and dignity of life; perils for the soul; perils for himself; perils for others also, if he be not advised and guided by others. A frivolous man never appreciates anything at its value; he treats the most serious, even the most holy, matters lightly; he jests, he foolishly laughs, at everything. Look at him; he has railed at such a man, such an action, such a virtue. Did he understand well what he did, what he said? No; but, nevertheless, he has said and he has done it; he has sent forth this raillery, this sarcasm, this satirical speech; has he foreseen where it may be borne? does he know that this speech is going, perhaps, like a keen arrow, to pierce a heart that he loves, bring discredit on one whom he esteems, compromise a work in which he is interested? how do we know, perhaps to scandalize and ruin a soul? No; he did not think of it; but, nevertheless, the words have been said and the injury perpetrated. How many of the accidents and misfortunes of life are the result of thoughtlessness and levity! They will say afterwards, "I did not dream of it." Well, it is precisely there they are wrong. Is it that it is not necessary to consider these matters? What is levity but absence of thought? and why have intelligence, reason, reflection, been given to him?

It is not necessary that levity, to create calamities, should be inspired by spitefulness; it may be met with in souls otherwise most talented; but it fetters, it paralyzes, it sometimes destroys the best gifts; when it comes in the way of great deeds, pure and tender acts, noble affections, nothing is more deplorable and more grievous to see. From levity springs frequently, without any interior malice, a spirit of playful scoffing, which prevents the earnest attention and deep penetration of the mind being brought to bear upon matters that most need being felt and deeply enjoyed. I say, without any evil intention — I mistake; for this levity necessarily implies a certain want of heart. A better heart, a stronger, a more elevated mind, would not have such levity. We can never, no, never, feel secure with respect to a frivolous man; we must tremble every moment, lest we see him commit some serious folly. Such a man does nothing so quickly as commit himself to a folly. He is unceasingly driven, by want of thought, precipitation, a moment of temper, a whim, a transport of passion, into indiscreet, imprudent steps, the consequences of which he has not calculated; he soon perceives that he has rashly entangled himself, taken a false course, placed himself in a wrong path; he sees it, but he is there — the evil is done. He has passed for a good priest, and a moment of forgetfulness has sufficed to make him lose his reputation, the fruits of his ministry, public confidence. He should have reflected, and said within himself, "Whither will this word reach? whither will this step, this connection, this companionship, this habit, lead me?" But the maxim of ancient philosophy, *In omnibus respice finem*, seems to have no existence for heedless souls; as incapable of reflection as of foresight or of resistance, they go on by chance, they follow an impulse, they give themselves up to a whim, a transport, an intoxication! Behold them accumulating imprudence upon imprudence, rashness upon rashness, folly upon folly! We may say, like a madman who recedes and dances on the brink of a precipice, or who balances himself on a swing, suspended by a thread, over an abyss, a spring seems to raise him to the sky; suddenly he falls back with all his weight into the abyss; this terrible play cannot last long. His head turns, he falls, and into what a gulf! This is the story of an infinite number of men and young people. Confide any serious affair to a thoughtless man, you may fear everything. He will compromise it by a thousand inadvertencies, and will infallibly cause it to fail. A frivolous man does not understand what responsibilities are; he does not see what the serious concern he is charged with claims from him, what he owes to it; and, instead of sacrificing to the serious business which he has to perform other matters less important, he will sacrifice all that is most serious to frivolities. Ah! the earnest man — the man who understands the bearing of matters, and treats them according to their bearing; who knows what it is to have a command, a mission, to be intrusted with a confidence, — and how much discretion, how much attention, how much diligence, and frequently even what sacrifices, the great affairs of life claim from him, — here is the man on whom we may count; but let us never count on a thoughtless soul, who does not attach to these matters the importance they merit, and does not know how to treat them with the discretion and the delicacy, with the application, the promptitude, the perseverance, and the devotion, they require.

And what danger if a frivolous man mix himself in the management of others! Now, unfortunately, it happens that men of character, incapable of guiding themselves, have — in consequence of their levity and this habit of not regarding matters seriously, of not weighing the gravity of duties — nevertheless the mania of meddling in the management of others, rashly advising and deciding with a peremptory tone, with as much self-possession as ignorance, and taking the helm in hand, without any mistrust of themselves, without suspecting even difficulties. What guides! "Woe," says the Scripture, "to the town whose prince is a child" — *Væ civitati cujus rex puer est!* He is an insane pilot who consults the weathercock of the vessel instead of the compass; who looks to the deceitful lights of the shore, instead of guiding himself by the regular course of the stars, following brilliant, but irregular, ephemeral meteors, and cannot avoid causing a shipwreck. And, if this levity be met with in a man whose office it is to direct souls, what a still greater misfortune!

Let youth, especially those being brought up for the priesthood, understand well — let those who are charged with their education not leave them ignorant — that the levities of early age cling to the man all his life, that he brings them everywhere with him. The priest, if he come into the world with this moral weakness, and if a firm, clerical education do not rid him of it, will carry it into the functions of his priesthood, into his most delicate relations with men, and even into that dreaded ministry, of which it is said, *Ars artium regimen animarum.* What a pastor, alas! what a director of souls, he will be! Behold whither levity of disposition may conduct one! And what is still more terrible for men of this stamp is, they are ignorant of the wrong they do to themselves and others; they have not even a suspicion of the faults they accumulate, the misfortunes they cause. By the deplorable habit which makes them treat everything lightly, even their souls, their conscience, their business, and their duties, and never seriously interrogate or examine themselves, they may find themselves without their knowledge in the most grievous state before God, and charged with the most dreadful responsibilities. So also, in life, they may allow themselves to be drawn farther than they would ever wish to go, if they had originally foreseen the consequences. Levity is usually the dupe and slave of the malice of others, who make use of it for their own ends; it is the instrument, and the culpable instrument, rather the first cause, of crime. We sometimes think that the unfortunates who give great scandals are perverse souls, villains. Well, no! Frequently they are but heedless, weak souls, who are found, in some delicate occasion, with strong passions unmortified, or who have been drawn on by others.

In the great French Revolution, notorious crimes were committed by thoughtless minds, directed by monsters. The worst of characters is that of not having one. Every one, except a sensible man, can make a frivolous man do all he wishes. It is right to say, that, in general, man is still more weak than corrupt; he almost always has more of levity than of malice. Do you believe, that, were it not for this terrible levity, a young man would have committed such an enormous fault? No; he has too good a heart, too upright a mind; but he did not reflect, and he could not resist. Do you, likewise, believe that this father, this mother, of a family, this honorable man, this magistrate, this priest, would, but for want of thought, but for levity, have fallen into such forgetfulness of himself and his duties? No; a thousand times no, never! Fatal levity, which conducts men into paths they would not wish to tread! which brings misfortune on families, shame on life, dishonor on religion! Fatal levity, which ruins more men even than wickedness does! Yet it must be said, however frivolous and superficial a soul may be, there is something grievously profound in it; it is the indestructible root of the three great concupiscences. Levity may cover them, but they are there, and one moment or other may break out; it is thus we see light, soft earth cover and secrete, under ephemeral flowers, infectious sinks and smouldering volcanoes. This dreadful peril must be averted by education at any price; pointed out and combated in every way by those whose task it is to bring up men for society and for the church.

It is that to which, I am happy to remark, the rule of an educational establishment is admirably suited; for it is rule that restrains and supports; it is rule that steadies these restless natures, which accustoms them to effort, obliges them to watch and conquer themselves; which gives them order, perseverance, constancy, self-possession, earnestness. But Christian fervor and piety, still more than rule, is supremely efficacious here. Indeed, solid piety gives to frivolous souls habits capable of counterbalancing and neutralizing, at least partly, this terrible defect; to wit, habits of reflection and habits of mortification. Hence, by the serious thoughts that a sincere practice of piety inspires, by the efforts it incites to and sustains, the two great deficiencies which give room to levity in a soul are supplied. And it is thus, as we have unceasingly stated, that piety is, in all things, the greatest resource of education — *Pietas ad omnia utilis est.*

But in order to make use of and sustain these two great and powerful means, to aid in the constant observation of rule, and to nourish fervent piety, that which is again and above all necessary here is the watchful, assiduous, paternal care of the masters. For if they do not follow attentively these poor natures of children, given up to themselves, they will make no progress in anything. And on the other hand, if I be permitted to say it, a very particular reason claims for thoughtless children these special cares. They are ill, and their malady has something less repulsive in it than haughty pride or shameful sensuality. The most interesting, the most amiable, class of invalids, still more to be pitied than blamed, how much of the tenderest interest becomes attached to those souls which rush on, inconsiderately and jestingly, to their ruin! How much of the most affectionate and most constant cares may be always lavished on them, and we may frequently have the consolation of seeing that these cares have not been useless!

CHAPTER XVII.

OF THE CHILD, AND OF THE RESPECT DUE TO THE LIBERTY OF HIS NATURE.

I HAVE said the child himself should labor, by a personal concurrence, by a free, spontaneous, generous action, in the great work of his education; it is the law of Nature and of Providence. This concurrence of the child is so necessary, that no education can be carried on without it; and no assistance, no foreign teacher, however clever and devoted he may be, can ever supply it. Whatever one may do, he will never bring up a child without himself, or in spite of himself. He must make him willing to be educated; he must cause him to do it for himself and by himself. This child is not a passive and inactive being, a shrub, a plant. No; he is an intelligent and thinking creature. Again, take care, the plant itself has an innate principle of vegetation, a sap, a germ, a root of life. It is but dead wood that can be shaped and fashioned without caution, without consulting it, without expecting anything of it. The child that you bring up is not a dead wood; he is a sublime being, capable of truth and virtue, of knowledge and love; he is an active, powerful, supreme creature: gifted with conscience and liberty, he should necessarily act in his own development.

This action, this concurrence, is essentially free; it may, it ought to be stimulated, sustained, encouraged; it ought not to be constrained or forced.

The beautiful and holy teachings of Christianity as to the liberty of man, as to his noble destiny, and the respect which is due to him, may be seriously and profoundly applied here. Indeed, the most active principle in the child, the most energetic, the most fertile for his education, is human liberty; yet on one condition; which is, that it be respected. Respected as is proper, governed without violence, directed with wisdom, the liberty, the personal action, of the child becomes, under the blessed influence of Divine Grace and the authority which presides over his education, the admirable resource, the soul, the life, of this entire education. In a word, as I have already had occasion to remark, in education what the teacher does himself is a trifling matter; what he causes to be done is everything: I mean that which he causes to be done freely. Once more, whosoever does not understand this, understands nothing of the work of human education.

The education of the son of Louis XIV., by Bossuet, offers a sad and memorable example of this. Bossuet wrote great works, admirable works, for the education of the Dauphin.[1] He did not make him do anything, not even indifferently, — the education was null. Without doubt, it was not the teacher was wanting to the pupil, but the pupil to the teacher.

[1] Among others, the "Discourse on Universal History" and "Sacred Politics."

Bossuet did not perceive it soon enough. The son of Louis XIV. had a vulgar nature; it was too magnificently cultivated: such elevated care and strong culture stifled it. Bossuet was too grand for him; and that great man was deceived here by his own genius; he labored for posterity while supposing he was laboring for that child. If Bossuet had had as much flexibility of mind and patience as he had strength and greatness, he would have descended to the level of that feeble intelligence; he would have caused it to do what it was capable of: that was not done, and we know the results. The memoirs of the time tell us, that the Dauphin, at more than forty years of age, son of that King of France whom the Emperors of Germany called "The King," and father of a King of Spain, passed entire days leaning on his elbows, his eyes fixed on a naked table, stopping his ears. His youth had thus flowed on under the teachings of Bossuet. He had been sensible of the presence of this immense genius only by the weariness and uneasiness that his early years and feeble nature experienced from it. The too powerful teacher had wearied and disheartened him. In the same manner, later on, the Dauphin lived in the grand age, and he only perceived it by the restraint and formality of his sad existence. This deplorable indifference accompanied him even to the end of his insignificant career. Such was the result of an education, where, according to the expression of Cardinal Beausset, "the teacher was everything, and the pupil nothing." Never has example proved in a more decisive manner what I said just now, and which I repeat, that in education, what the teacher does is a trifling matter; what he causes to be done is everything. I always understand what he causes to be done freely. No doubt, evil must be repressed; but never force nor compel one violently to be good; it is otherwise no longer good. Stimulate, dispose, exhort them to be good; but never force them. Violent constraint in education, as elsewhere, injures the development of nature; that is to say, the very work it should perform well. If there are so few successful educations, it is because there are so few really free, spontaneous, generous, as it is fitting they should be. I do not fear to say, the great evil of education in France, during these fifty years, is, that it is deficient in freedom. The liberty of the child is not respected. Intellectual liberty, moral liberty, all is constrained.

The law of Nature, the law of Providence, everything, is despised. Have we not heard the present century proclaim and set up in principle this strange assertion, that French youth ought to be cast in a mould, and struck like a piece of money with the same effigy? I have already had the opportunity of refuting these sad words and the fatal error contained in them, no doubt unknown to those who uttered them; but I will say frankly, the more I meditate on them, the less I comprehend them; the more they obscure, in my eyes, all that is noble, elevated, ideal, delicate, free, divine, in the work of education. I find the vulgarity of this image repugnant to our beautiful French tongue. And, nevertheless, is it not there? What have they tried to realize with violence among us? It is not alone the liberty of families, their primitive and inviolable rights,[1] that have been despised; it is also, it is especially, the liberty and sacred rights of childhood. As for me, I declare, while I can occupy myself, at home or abroad, with the education of youth, I will respect human liberty still more religiously in the smallest child than in the grown man; because this latter will, at least, know how to defend himself against me; the child cannot. No; never will I outrage childhood to the extent of considering it as a matter that I can cast in a mould, in order that it should come out with the imprint my will would give it.

The child, regarding him from our point of view, is man himself; the depositary of all the gifts, all the hopes, all the dawning powers, of humanity, clothed with every grace, every energy, every human dignity. Behold what must be respected! But you say, He is so weak! It is a serious error; you do not know him; he is stronger than you. Besides, were he as weak as you say, he should still be, his weakness especially should be, respected. His power, also, must be respected. It is not to be despised. This child, weak as he is, may conquer you. You can strike him, you can crush him; he is not conquered; it is you who are: his will, his soul, invincibly resist you; and you have done nothing but a stupid and barbarous action! As for him, he will despise and hate you. And what can you do to hinder him from despising and hating you? I un-

[1] M. Guizot.

derstand you; you reply to me, that you have the resource of hating and despising him in your turn. That is much; but what will you gain by it? You will, on account of his money, perhaps, continue to bring him up; but, when the youth of a great country shall have been brought up in this fashion, what will the country gain by it? No; I have hardly ever seen a greater display of moral force than that which the weakest children have exerted against those of their masters, who knew only how to constrain them with violence in their childhood. There are sometimes in these young souls depths of contempt, frightful in their simplicity and justice. It is, of all human contempts, that which I should least wish to face.

From the beginning of my priesthood, Providence devoted me to the work of education. The chief sentiment that I then brought into the accomplishment of my duties towards children was a warm affection for their age; I loved them tenderly; I could not meet a child of twelve years old without experiencing an involuntary emotion; without thinking how happy I should be if I were called to cultivate his mind and his heart; if I could teach him to love God and virtue, and, especially, prepare him for his first Communion. To-day, after twenty-five years of devotion to this work, when I ask myself, What is the most profound sentiment that I have carried away from it and preserve? I discover it is the sentiment of respect for childhood. Yes; what I particularly learned during these pleasant and laborious years is to respect children. I will say more, — and those of them who may read these pages will not take offence at these words, when they shall have well understood them, — I have learned to fear them. The respect with which any child, whatsoever he may be, inspires me at present, and I feel this impression is henceforth ineffaceable in my soul, is a religious respect, mixed with fear, at the sight of these young and powerful creatures, whose faculties are so free, so strong, so invincible. This sentiment has become almost a weakness of mind and character in me. But no; I am wrong in saying it; there is no trace of weakness here. It is true, I can no longer see a child of three years without experiencing a certain terror, without reflecting profoundly on him, without considering that his will is independent of mine. Actually, young as he is, he can exercise his will without me, in spite of me, against me. He may be killed, but he cannot be compelled to will in spite of himself. What is he to speak of — a child of three years? and what matters three years more or less? He has my nature, he has yours; he is human nature entire. He is a superior being, gifted like you and me; your likeness and mine, a power equal to ours. Ah! you count this child as nothing; he amuses you; you play with his rising will; you constrain it without reason, or you yield to it without prudence. Well, in this dreaded play you will be vanquished, and you will learn sooner or later, at your own expense, what a fault it is to treat a child with levity, and without respect, or rather with harshness, and without love. As for me, I do not know of a greater disorder, and I willingly repeat this speech of a philosopher: "No; there is no being more delicate and more sensitive; no one whose guidance requires more profound art; no one who must be treated with more caution or regard."

Faults, errors, in this respect, may be numerous, infinitely varied, unfelt, unperceived, and almost always past remedy. I will try to point out some of them. There is at first a rock to avoid, which one in a measure draws near, as he makes greater efforts to attain the end he wishes to arrive at. Education is, indisputably, a great work — a work of perfection; it is indisputably a supreme type that we must seek to realize in this work; but even that is a great danger. The finest theories, the most perfect plans, the strictest rules, those containing the most absolute perfection, are not the most difficult to be found; but, on account of being perfect, they become impracticable and injurious. What is essential, and what is very difficult to secure, is this even temperament; to quote St. Paul, this "sobriety of perfection," without which all theories, all rules, are deficient in wisdom.

It is still more necessary to spare the weakness of the child than to draw from him all the fruits he is capable of producing. It is always a great fault to force Nature; she resists and breaks, or rather she gives way, and becomes weakened. Moreover, the constraint of excessive perfection is always injurious to the real strength and development of character; one becomes disgusted with that which he has for a long time been forced to be in spite of himself; and one hour of freedom has frequently destroyed the ephemeral labor of many years. There are two equally pernicious methods of corrupting nature and depraving children. They become as grievously perverted by oppression as by spoiling. Let teachers of youth not forget that indulgence towards children is always nearer to justice than severity is; alas! and with men also; for, if children are little men, it must be acknowledged men are often grown children. When one devotes himself to the work of education, he requires an inexhaustible fund of indulgence. This indulgence is equity itself. Every one ought always, in the words of the Church, be *memor conditionis suæ.* Let us never forget what we were, not only at their age, but what we are in more advanced age. No doubt, also, there are simple and fixed principles on which all good education is founded, and which may be always followed, while keeping to the lessons of experience and the lights of a sound philosophy. But though these principles may be unchangeable, and to swerve from them in the bringing up youth be necessarily vicious, it is not the less true that the disposition of every child — what the hand of Providence has placed in him — his tastes, and his different capacities, must be studied. It is not less true, that each must be brought up for the state to which he is called, and, at an early age, given habits that will one day render it easy for him to fulfil his duties. We have said, and nothing is more certain, even as in medicine there is no universal remedy for all maladies, all constitutions, so also the science of teaching cannot give uniform rules for every character. The great principle which rules and enlightens everything here is, that education ought to follow and aid nature, never violently to restrain or force it: and for this reason, though immutable in its higher principles, education ought to infinitely vary its action, its means, and its forms. There is nothing which education ought to have more aversion to, more horror of, than the common type, the mould in which all natures are violently cast. Fénelon says somewhere, "Where will you find two faces which wholly resemble each other?" The minds of men are not less different than their faces. Education, which is to improve nature, and whose glory it is to co-operate in the work of Providence, ought not to have less variety in all that it performs than nature and Providence Himself; it ought to adapt itself to all characters, take the forms of all minds, and find, in the treasures of its devotion and its power, wherewith to bring them up, wherewith to mould them with different and new features every day. In a word, education is a work of infinite variety; nothing is less suitable to it than narrow and uniform views, harsh measures, inflexible means, forced action. Its general principles, its great laws, are unchangeable; but the application perpetually varies, and, on that account, gives birth in a higher degree to the absolute perfection to which education should aspire. I sometimes said to my worthy fellow-laborers, "An educational establishment is a sphere of intellectual activity and immense thought. The centre is immovable; the foundation of its principles is unchangeable; but from thence springs an action of never-ending variety, which becomes extended, restrained, modified, renewed, according to the different natures on which it is exercised, and of which it seems to take every form, in the same moment that it takes possession of, and moulds them like to the supreme type. It even takes possession of them only on condition of being transformed into them; like a virtue, a precious essence, which takes the different forms of the vases of gold, of iron, or of clay, that it is poured into; or rather like the grace[1] of God itself, which submits to different transformations, suiting itself to the heart into which God causes it to flow. Divine grace penetrates, strengthens, vases of clay. Sometimes it converts them into vases of gold. It softens, it polishes, vases of iron, and renders them as brilliant as solid. It labors to transform all into vases of honor."[2] However suitable these comparisons of the Holy Scriptures may be, it remains to be said, that education can only succeed in forming souls, according to the variety and nature of their talents, by continually varying in power, weight, dimension, form, position, method, and action, all its resources. To act otherwise is to submit the child to an intellectual, moral, physical constraint; and sometimes even a religious constraint, which throws his faculties into a profound perturbation; changes and imbitters his nature; and frequently goes to the extent of causing him to reject far from him, as an odious yoke and an insupportable tyranny, all the cares of a forced and constrained education.

[1] Multiformis gratia Dei. —*St. Paul.*

[2] Vasa aurea. . . . . . . Vas in honorem. —*Ibid.*

CHAPTER XVIII.

THE CHILD; THE RESPECT DUE TO THE LIBERTY OF HIS INTELLECT.

THERE are many important aspects under which the education of the child, and the respect due to the dignity of his nature, may be particularly considered. I will try to point out, successively, how fatal are moral, intellectual, and even physical constraint, to education. And let it not be thought that intellectual constraint can be less fatal. I have seen disastrous consequences from it, and I ought to mention them here. I have already spoken of the culpable weakness of some parents, who do not regard sacrificing the instruction of the mind, and moral education itself, to the effeminacy and the physical cares of their children. I ought to speak here of quite another defect: I mean the haughty hardness of other parents, and the odious cupidity of too great a number of teachers, who, in order to obtain for their own name the glory of prizes at competitions, or the honor of brilliant examinations, condemn poor children to labor without relaxation the whole day and part of the night during entire months, thus causing those weak bodies and those organs, that nature has not yet strengthened, to succumb under the weight of continued fatigue. I have seen young people, brilliantly gifted, who, from excessive labor at too early an age, had been reduced to impotence — to intellectual imbecility — all their lives.

In former times, Plutarch wrote these remarkable words respecting this: "I know some fathers who are really enemies of their children. Ambitious of seeing them make the most rapid progress, and obtain an extraordinary superiority in everything, they overload them with a forced labor, the weight of which crushes them. The result is a discouragement which renders the sciences hateful to them. Plants moderately watered grow easily; but too great an abundance of water stifles the germ in them. Thus it is the soul becomes nourished and strengthened by well-managed labor; excess overwhelms it, and extinguishes its faculties." The father of Blaise Pascal had entirely opposite ideas, and pursued a very different method in the education of his family. His daughter, Jacqueline Pascal, relates that this wise father, in bringing up Blaise, and applying him to study, followed the principle of always keeping the child below what he was capable of. Let us study, in the memoirs of the time, what the educations of Fénelon, Bossuet, M. Olier, were; we shall see therein an admirable tempering of the strength of labor and caution for the weakness of early age; a clever mixture of prudence and eagerness, grave condescension and prudent austerity. It was thus that all those great men who regenerated France during the first half of the seventeenth century, and prepared all the splendor of the reign of Louis the

Fourteenth, were brought up. We have said education is, without doubt, essentially progressive; but we have also said its method of proceeding should never be violent, nor its progress hastened; the child will not bear it; his liberty will be injured, and even the foundation of nature impaired: his physical, intellectual, moral, and religious development is necessarily a work of time and patience. If you wish to make a man of this child, it is necessary to labor at it, — as Providence itself did, — with respect, with time, with gentleness. You will otherwise disturb this soul; you will yourself defeat your whole work, and your most ardent efforts will but remove you farther than ever from the goal. It is in order to arrive more surely there, and by an idea of the highest wisdom, that education has, as we have seen, been divided into three different periods; namely, maternal education, primary education, secondary education. Unfortunately, this wise and progressive tardiness is not always observed. One of the most frequent of intellectual constraints, and the most deserving of compassion, is that of forcibly engaging poor children in the study of ancient languages, for which they have but little taste, indifferent capacity, and, besides, in which they are not offered any real help to aid them in the success of so difficult a labor. I believe, and I unhesitatingly proclaim, that the study of three languages, of three great literatures — French, Greek, and Latin — is the most powerful means we have for the highest intellectual education; but still the mind must be capable of it. Now, among those who make their classes without making their studies, in our establishments for public instruction, how many of them are there absolutely incapable of doing anything else! How many are there, in consequence of Greek and Latin, condemned to ignorance and stupidity, through the deplorable carelessness of which they are the victims! When sixty, eighty, and sometimes a hundred, are crowded into one class, is there any possibility whatsoever of these unfortunates studying or succeeding? What do all others, save those prepared for competition, become, and what can they become? Who occupies himself with them? Who can occupy himself with them? The most zealous professor is obliged to leave them languishing in the most deplorable neglect of all labor. He asks but one thing of them; it is, not to move, to be silent. Silence and immobility are the conditions of peace and existence for them. It is necessary that they be as if they were not there; however, they are condemned to be there, and that for the space of ten years, ten of the most ardent years of their mettlesome youth! Those unfortunate beings will thus pass all the long hours of their sad days, becoming pale over authors they do not and cannot understand; reading, or at least having forced under their eyes, books they will never comprehend; writing themes in which there is neither sense nor any form of human thought or speech, and that at the epoch when all the most active faculties of the mind ought to be developed in them. How can one not see that it is making them submit to the most brutal intellectual tyranny that ever existed? Speaking only of their studies, would you wish to know what they become with such a system? Here is what the professor of philosophy, in one of the most important *lycées* of France, published a short time ago with respect to the average of university studies: "This average is now so low, that the question is, Can it be still lowered? Everywhere, even in Paris, whither our habits of centralization despatch every year the most brilliant subjects from the provinces, the medium of the classes is deplorably weak. In Paris there is an abyss between the first five or six and the rest of the class; there is another between the ten following and what is called the tail of the class. Now, this tail is interminable; so much so, that there is no serious difference between the twentieth and the sixtieth. The sixtieth is at zero, the twentieth is infinitely low. It is the same thing in the departments, except that the class is decapitated of the five or six choice pupils included in the Parisian *lycées*, and who seem to absorb for their own benefit all the sap of the university. This statement becomes verified in the most irrefragable and grievous manner at the examination for the degree of Bachelor of Arts. The faculties are not very exacting; and, nevertheless, the proportion of candidates refused for not knowing how to translate passably is really formidable. As to the oral examinations, I pray, with all my heart, that God may never lead a German or an Englishman there to witness them; or, at least, that he will spare my national self-love the sorrow and humiliation of finding myself beside him. I have not courage to say more regarding them; they can be witnessed." Why should we be surprised that studies thus carried on, that such teaching, should have inspired so many minds among us, otherwise distinguished, with a supreme contempt and a sort of horror for Greek and Latin? I do not speak strongly enough; among many this sentiment goes to the extent of a contempt and horror of books and all literary instruction. I could quote here a multiplicity of my experiences.[1]

How many young people, how many men, among us, whose lamentable story this is! I am going to speak of those who have neither taste nor marked capacity for Greek or Latin, and whom a system of necessary and frightful neglect condemns to annihilation. I ought to speak of those whose culture has not been neglected, whom teachers worthy of the name exert themselves to instruct, but who, through viciousness and ingratitude of mind, are incapable of the instruction they are compelled to receive. This

[1] I knew, I still know, one of the cleverest of our architects, who had the misfortune of undergoing in his childhood this odious constraint. However, he ended by shaking off the yoke; and his parents came to the decision, in spite of the advice of his masters, of breaking up the course of what they called his studies, and setting him to the art of drawing, for which he had a remarkable taste and talent. "It is that which has saved me," said he to me; "but for it, I was morally and intellectually ruined. I acknowledge, even though unwillingly, I preserved for a long time an instinctive dislike to books, for which I blushed; but I have had much to do; pardon this remembrance and this language." He then said to me, smiling, "Fifteen years were necessary to remove the disgust the college had inspired in me for books and haricots. I hated one as much as the other; and it was only last year that I could eat haricots without repugnance, and read with pleasure a translation of Virgil."

is again a great misfortune. We have, without exception, a sad and notorious instance of this kind in an education of which I have already had occasion to speak, that of the Grand Dauphin. Madame de Maintenon[1] wrote, "The late Monseigneur, at five or six years old, knew a thousand Latin words, and not one when he was his own master." Madame de Caylus wrote,[2] "The harsh manner with which he was compelled to study gave him so great a disgust for books, that he formed the resolution never to open one when he should be his own master; he has kept his word." But people will say to me, What is to be done with those children incapable of, and who display absolutely no taste, no talent, for, the study of languages or literature? What did you do yourself with them?—for doubtless you must have met with them. The answer is very simple; it is necessary to study their nature; to seek out, to discover, what they are capable of, and apply them to it, without reference to the ordinary rules and general methods of instruction; it is what I have many times had occasion to do, or advise enlightened parents to do. Though languages and letters may be the most powerful means of intellectual education, there are others which have their value also. I shall explain this in detail when I shall treat of high literary education. At present it is sufficient for me to say, that a child must be applied only to the studies for which he has capacity; it is necessary to give his education a possible foundation; to labor at his in-

[1] To Madame de Ventadour, June 16, 1715.
[2] Souvenir de Madame de Caylus.

tellectual development in a medium that will not stifle it. All this is the plainest good sense. Every other mode of action is revolting; and, lest these words should appear very severe, I will add, that in my eyes there is so criminal an abuse of authority in it, that I do not know anything which affects me more sorrowfully. The committing of such violence to a child, to his liberty, and the weakness of his nature, has always inspired me with real horror. I ought to point out here another constraint imposed on the greater number of children among us, and to which persons generally wish to close their eyes. I speak of the simultaneous study of French[1] and Latin, to which they are sometimes at the tenderest age condemned; it is, even for the most talented children, truly odious intellectual tyranny, the consequences of which are frequently lamentable; and, nevertheless, what is more usual? How is it we do not see that the simultaneous study of two so different grammars, to which, through a superabundance of zeal, the Greek grammar is sometimes added, crushes these young minds, overturns their memory, disturbs and embarrasses their whole intellectual development? How can we wish to see these little intellects becoming ruined by these fantastic conflicts of heterogeneous declinations, of conjugations without relation, of nouns and articles? How can you maintain that syntaxes, methods, rules so opposite in themselves, will appear simple and intelligible to them, and that they will assign to each

[1] In this country we should read, "of English." — *Note of Translator.*

object its part and its place? But though they should have only this multitude of words, signifying the same thing, and having no resemblance, must it not be more than they could do to retain either one or the other? Do we not know that it is almost impossible, at this age, to take in analogies, comprehend general relations, abstract dissimilarities, because a child does not judge, compare, nor deduce, hardly reasons? Simple ideas or comparisons are necessary for him; and besides, what would his terms of comparison be? Until then he knows only what his own language has been on a level with, and made use of to express his early wants; he scarcely sees farther. Does not the most ordinary good sense demand that his mind be first strengthened; that he be made to understand, as perfectly as possible, his mother-tongue, which he already speaks and comprehends, in which at least he is not thrown into a barbarous and unknown region? And then, when he shall suitably possess this tongue, when he shall have well taken in the general principles, the grammar, the syntax, the method, and the orthography, it will be no longer a labor and an embarrassment to him, but an instrument, a means, a power, for studying, for conquering another. It is the want of observing and understanding these matters, so simple, that causes this tender age, so deserving of some mercy, to be still so cruelly tormented. And to what does it tend? To disgust it, sometimes for ever, with study; or, at least, grievously retard the first steps in its career. I ask again, of what use are the eighth, ninth, and even tenth classes, in which these poor children pine for years? Whoever has followed closely these wretched classes, whoever has seen with his own eyes the weariness, the disgust, of the masters, the despair and torture of the pupils, will, without any doubt, share my opinion regarding them. As for me, my experience once gained, my resolution was soon taken, and immutable; from that time, whatever might be even the prayers of the parents, I never consented to admit into the *Petit Seminaire* of Paris any children not suitably prepared by a solid primary instruction to receive secondary instruction. To place by force in the hands of these unhappy children the three grammars, French, Greek, and Latin, to compel them to apply themselves simultaneously to them, appeared odious to me; again, it was in my eyes an intolerable abuse of paternal and magisterial authority. But you will ask me, What did you do, then? Something very simple. For example, I sent these young children to the house of the good Brothers of the Christian Doctrine, at Passy; they remained there two or three years, occupied only with primary instruction; and, when they were afterwards brought back to me, they then commenced with greater facility to study the Latin and Greek grammars. They had no longer the disgust of pining whole years over the principles of grammar, which they had successfully studied in their mother-tongue; all the preliminary and general notions were known beforehand. No confusion remained in their minds; their dawning faculties had been suitably cultivated and strengthened by natural exercise in an idom which they understood easily, and listened to with pleasure. Moreover, and uncommon enough, they knew how to read and write correctly, even from dictation. In fine, their minds were already adorned with much accessory knowledge of history, geography, arithmetic, and even drawing. In a word, they were children really instructed in everything they ought to know; they replied to all my questions with confidence. I read in the vivacity of their looks the happy certainty that they had acquired their little knowledge, and their eagerness to conquer more. And when at length I admitted them to study the humanities, when I declared them deserving and capable of it, when the Latin and Greek languages were placed before them, it was a pleasure, honor, and not a torture, to them; it was, as it were, opening a new field to their young minds; it was a brilliant conquest proposed to their ardor. From eight to ten, eleven, or thereabout, they had received good primary instruction. From ten or eleven to sixteen or seventeen, they passed easily and gloriously through the whole course of the humanities; from sixteen, eighteen, or nineteen, their intellectual education was completed by the study of the sciences and philosophy. In fine, at eighteen, nineteen, or twenty, these young people were ready for everything; and, save one or two exceptions, I have never known them to be refused at their examinations. It was thus I acted whenever the wisdom of parents permitted me, and it is thus we should always act. Such a course renders a considerable service to youth, to families, to the country, and will cause this tyrannical and besotting system, which I have pointed out, to disappear, and with it those sad classes, called the tenth, ninth, and eighth, which are but a lost and hateful time for children, after which they know neither Latin, Greek, nor French, and, besides, become especially incapable of learning, of knowing, anything else. But I may be asked, Do you wish to modify profoundly the general system and universal order of studies? No; I wish but for two matters: Firstly, that a professor be a sincere, honest, compassionate man, and not retain in his class fifty or sixty pupils with whom he does not and cannot occupy himself, and who are becoming stupefied; that poor children, without taste, inclination, preparation, or before the time they shall be capable of it, be not condemned to study the learned languages. Moreover, I consider that writing, reading, the grammar of their own language, elementary and universal history, geography, fables, drawing, music, the elements of arithmetic, the simplest and most interesting ideas of the natural sciences, can and ought to occupy more agreeably and more usefully the first years of youth, than the study of Greek and Latin. I do not wish to modify anything in the system of the humanities; it is here simply a question of order and time. I would confine myself to delaying the study of Latin for a year, or even two. I would commence later, but in order to finish sooner. This study, coming in due time, would be more easy, more prompt, and more certain; the delay would be found more speedily repaired. Not only can they acquire it better, and more of it, but they can acquire it more quickly. And in that way, without interfering with the general system of the humanities, I would but happily uproot and overturn a bad routine, a barbarous habit, which favors, at the expense of this age, so deserving of compassion, the negligence of some, and cupidity of others. The study of mathematics has also become among us one of the most unfortunate of intellectual constraints; I ought to point out the dangers of it. People are sometimes surprised at seeing certain pupils of our trained schools, of the *Polytechnique* itself, tending to a deplorable mediocrity in every respect. I am never surprised at it. The laws of weak nature, in these young people, undergo the inevitable consequences of the premature instruction forced upon them. They have been applied to the study of the exact sciences before their mind, being sufficiently developed and strengthened, was capable of it; they have not been able to sustain the weight; mathematics have crushed them; so far from being brought up by their education, they have not even been instructed; they have been dried up, exhausted, and ruined forever. In order to understand this well, it is necessary to recollect that the faculties of man cannot ripen nor become wholly developed but according to the laws of a successive and measured progression. It does not enter into the order of Providence that they should all attain at the same time their strength, their maturity, their natural power. We therefore see memory first appearing, imagination then revealing itself, moral feeling afterwards. Nothing is more tardy in children than thought. They have certain natural ideas; but these are almost always ideas which spring from their imagination; nothing is more rare among them than connected thought and purely intellectual operations. Connected thought, whether it be abstract or complex, almost always confounds them; in a word, reflection is singularly weak in them, judgment very indifferent, and consecutive reasoning nearly impossible. In that state of things, what comes to pass? Mathematics are frequently too great, too difficult, a study for these young pupils. Without any doubt, mathematics, by a useful and vigorous exercise, by laborious intellectual gymnastics, strengthen and perfect reflection, judgment, reasoning; but they absolutely exact that these faculties shall already have acquired a certain vigor, a certain development; otherwise they crush them. Experience, in this respect, has always led me to the same conclusion. I have always observed, every time a premature or absorbing predominance in education has been granted to mathematics, that great misfortunes resulted from it: sensibility, imagination, these two noble and brilliant faculties, companions of reason, become grievously extinguished; you mutilate, sometimes in a frightful manner, that amiable nature; you impair its moral dignity as well as its intellectual power. Mathematics, when studied before their time, actually injure even those faculties which they exercise at the expense of the two others; for, in extinguishing these latter, they deprive the former of all the assistance they might expect from their companions; and reason itself becomes dried up without being more strengthened. Moreover, as mathematics most frequently exercise the accuracy of the mind only on geometrical and material abstractions, they disturb, and sometimes even impair, moral feeling, if it be not very strong in the soul. Not only do they rob the intellect of the grace, the brilliancy, the generosity, the warmth, which imagination would have communicated to it, but they deprive it also of moral exactness, that is to say, real greatness of soul, and all that is noble in the human intellect. I have said, and maintain, these are great misfortunes; yes, it is a great misfortune for a young man and his family. What do they gain by it in the end? They sometimes make one mathematician more, but frequently, also, a man less. And, as I indicated farther back, we are frequently condemned to regret the absence of both. Certainly I am not one of those who despise human science and learned schools. The Polytechnic has rendered great services to our country, and we may be proud of its professors. Yes, learned men are worthy of every encouragement, and of being nobly rewarded for intelligence and labor. I have always respectfully admired these great and generous minds, whose most profound investigations, whose powerful calculations, have mounted to the heavens, and descended to the bottom of the abysses; whose wonderful discoveries extend to the most distant ages, penetrate all nature, and unveil her most hidden secrets. I willingly cry out, *Felix qui potuit rerum cognoscere causas!* I willingly render solemn homage to Laplace, Bertholet, Lavoisier, Cuvier, and so many others. I pause; for, in speaking of the dead,

I draw too near to the living, and I do not wish to wound their modesty by my praises. But it is precisely my admiration for those names, great in science, and my respect for science itself, which causes me to require that it be not debased by delivering it to young minds still unworthy of it, and incapable of raising an intelligent and sensible glance to its beautiful light. Science, which ought to enlighten them, stupefies and blinds them then; after these deplorable and impotent attempts, those poor young people are often condemned to fix but weakened and stupid eyes, and the uncertain glance of an extinguished or wandering intellect, on literature and human science. Besides, I cannot forget that the princes of science, and the greatest philosophical geniuses, have thought and spoken on this grave subject as I do. These astounding words of Descartes were recently quoted to me: "The study of mathematics renders one unfit for that of philosophy." I myself read in the works of that great man, "There is nothing more empty than occupying one's self with numbers and imaginary figures, as if one wished to arrest his knowledge with such trifles, and, by applying himself with so much care to these superficial demonstrations, to give up, in a manner, the use of his reason." [1]

[1] Here is what the learned author of the Life of Descartes recounts: "His own experience had a long time before convinced him of how little utility mathematics were, especially when they were cultivated only for themselves, without application to other matters. From the year 1620, he had entirely neglected the rules of arithmetic. His attachment to geometry subsisted a little longer in his heart; but we may say it had already fallen away in 1623, if it be true, that, in

Who does not know the distinction made by Pascal between the spirit of exactness and the spirit of geometry? Every one has read in his "Thoughts" the well-known passage, where, in exalting the merits of geometry, he mocks geometry which is only geometry, and finds it ridiculous, false, and insupportable, because it wishes to treat delicate matters geometrically. Leibnitz, also, has expressed his sentiments on this subject with all the gravity and usual elevation of his views. After having spoken of the epoch in which some celebrated authors turned their attention towards the study of nature and mathematics, he adds, "This is not the place to explain in what this kind of study now appears to me defective, and how it happens that the disciples of some of those great men, though surrounded by so much assistance, nevertheless did not perform

1638, he professed that he had neglected geometry for more than fifteen years" (p. 402, vol. iii., of his Letters). "He was not surprised at seeing the greater number of clever men, even those of the most solid genius, not delay in neglecting or rejecting, as foolish and puerile amusements, sciences of this kind, as soon as they had made their first essays in them. He found nothing which appeared to him really less substantial than occupying one's self with purely simple numbers and imaginary figures, as if one ought to keep to these trifles without carrying his views farther. He saw they were even something more than useless, and he believed it was dangerous to apply one's self too seriously to these superficial demonstrations, arrived at more frequently by chance than by industry or experience, and which appeal to the eyes and the imagination rather than the understanding. His maxim was, that this application caused us insensibly to give up using our reason, and exposed us to lose the path its light had traced out for us (De Directione ingenii, reg. 4). These are partly the motives which induced him to give up pure mathematics." — (Baillet, Hist. of Descartes, p. 111, art. 12, edit. of 1691, book ii. chap. vi.)

anything worth commemorating. I shall merely remark, that, since this period, the study of antiquity and solid erudition has, in some manner, fallen into contempt." — (Letters of Leibnitz to M. Huet, Bishop of Avranches.) Bossuet held the same opinion, and expressed it in his own way, in a letter dated May 21st, 1687, addressed to a young mathematician: "Do you believe, sir, it follows that one can be very capable of taking part in matters relating to theology because he has a knowledge of physics and algebra, or even understands some of the general truths of metaphysics?" Fénelon spoke still more energetically: "Mistrust," said he, "the bewitchery and diabolical attractions of geometry." — (Vol. v., p. 514, Correspondence.) He did not wish the Duke of Burgundy to study too much mathematics, lest they should cause him to lose infinite time in foolish researches, and render him too angular. — (Correspondence and Memoirs of the Education of the Duke of Burgundy.) Certainly, after such authorities and such reasons, I may be permitted to add in conclusion, It is a great misfortune for a nation when a thoughtless impulse gives to mathematics, before their time, a predominance in the studies of youth; if these studies be successful, we may perhaps have a great number of accurate geometricians and useful engineers; but we may also have a great number of men with indifferent talents.[1] One class of

[1] France had already, early in the beginning of this century, gained a first and deplorable experience of it. Here is what M. de Poirson, one of the most eminent members of the corps of instruction, publishes: "From this new plan of public teaching, in which

training will pass for the highest intellectual culture of the country; it will be forgotten that there is an exactness and elevation of view, which are not alone the elevation of mathematics and the exactness of trigonometry, profoundly desirable in human society. All ambition, every effort, is being turned to this side; each year many thousands of young minds, from thirteen to eighteen, shall be condemned to interrupt all intellectual and moral education, all development of thought and language, in order to devote themselves only to algebra and geometry. We shall see them, each year, present themselves for examinations almost impossible for every one; some hundreds of candidates will with great trouble be received, and all the others will fall back on themselves disheartened, on their mutilated studies, their weakened faculties, their exhausted youth, their ruined future. But what is to be done? Will it be necessary to close all those schools which prepare for so many

mathematical sciences predominate, results the most instantaneous, the most deplorable, and most easily perceived, are produced. Within six years, almost all youth have become shamefully ignorant. Some private schools, though exceptions, still nourish feeble remains of enlightenment; in all other parts of France they have become extinct. In the year 1800, the pupils of the special government schools who had passed their twentieth year apprised an astounded country that some of its subjects prepared to enter the public offices would be found unfit for the position in consequence of deficiency in literary knowledge, being unable to render their ideas into language, to express themselves in a clear and correct manner, or produce an intelligible report without faults of orthography. It was not the empire of intelligence alone which was menaced in our country." (Collection of Laws and Rules regarding Public Instruction, vol. i. pp. 37, 38, 46, 47.—Explanation of the Reasons for the Law of 1802, by Fourcray, vol. ii. p. 62.—Fourcy's History of the Polytechnic School, p. 214.)

important public services, in which, each year, are recruited for the artillery, the naval service, the mines, the public works, naval construction, etc., men designed to put in motion, to give direction to those great works? Without doubt, no; but what should be done is, to retard sufficiently the period of admission to these schools, in order that the young people who aspire to it can be brought up to the altitude of science without being crushed before their time by labors beyond their strength. Here is what should be done, and I affirm what no one can dispute. All will then go on better: we shall not have less learning; on the contrary, we shall have more real learning, and an ardent and generous youth will no longer be compelled to submit the liberty of its tastes, and the most legitimate of its dislikes, to the most hateful intellectual constraint that has ever been imagined.

CHAPTER XIX.

OF THE CHILD, AND THE RESPECT DUE TO THE LIBERTY OF HIS WILL.

I HAVE pointed out the dangers of intellectual constraint — those of moral constraint are still more to be dreaded. Certainly it seems hardly possible, that in a country, in an age, like ours, the moral liberty of youth can be seriously menaced. At the same time, let us not be in a hurry to trust to appearances; we shall, perhaps, be cruelly deceived by them. There may possibly be many errors in this respect; and I have seen some results so disastrous, that I may be permitted at least to point them out rapidly. I will first say, that good educations, the most careful, the best carried on, have always had to guard against themselves. Fénelon asks, "What do we see in the greater number of educations? No liberty, no enjoyment, always lessons, silence, a cramping posture, correction, and threats." He adds, "An exactitude and a seriousness, of which those who require them would not themselves be capable, are often demanded from children." Again he says, "Those who govern children will excuse nothing in them, and everything in themselves." Let it be understood, then, this is not an idle dissertation; nothing is more practical, more important, and I believe more useful, at the present, than to recall the principles which govern the question. If education be, as we have seen, a work essentially founded on authority and respect, it is also essentially a work of human liberty; for religious and moral education is not, and never can be, a work of constraint and violence. Without doubt, it is necessary that authority should be grave and firm at bottom; but it is also necessary that its action should be mild and pliant, in accordance with the admirable expression of the Holy Scriptures: *Attingens ad finem fortiter, suaviterque disponens omnia.*

Plato speaks of the different threads which ought to enchain us in life. He says, "There are some of iron, which are tight and hard; but there is one which is of gold, and full of gentleness; it is the thread of reason. I willingly admit that education ought to have the pliancy and strength of a chain of gold, which leaves to him whom it retains the freedom of his movements, and makes itself felt by him only at a moment when he may be in danger of swerving from good or precipitating himself into evil." No doubt it is necessary that children be stimulated, but without violence, by their moral education. It must check them without constraining them; in a word, it is necessary that children be free, under the powerful, active, and vigilant action of education. It is necessary to know how to induce, restrain, arrest, or direct their will, form their conscience and their heart, without forcing them or impairing their nature. This is what Quintilian formerly expressed by this speech: *Studium discendi, voluntate, quæ cogi non potest, constat*—"Study, virtue, education, depend on the will not being constrained." It is necessary to make them desire, choose freely, and love goodness, truth, justice, honesty, greatness. I say freely, for Fénelon says, "One does not love only in as much as it pleases him to love." In order to succeed in this, it is necessary to enter into the depths of the hearts of those children; it is necessary to have the key to them; every spring must be set in motion; they must be persuaded; mild insinuation and paternal cares are necessary; it must be by a father or mother; in a word, the great art of educating souls, that of making one's self loved, and winning confidence, is required in order to succeed in persuading. It is necessary to understand that this task has an antipathy to all anger, impatience, harshness, and severity; dry and absolute authority, military discipline, the material force of which I speak just now, will never accomplish it. Ah! without doubt, as Fénelon said again, it is more easy to reprehend than to persuade; it is shorter to threaten than to instruct; it is easier for haughtiness and human impatience to strike those who resist them, than to bend mildly to the voice of reason. But what comes to pass by that? Every one becomes silent, every one endures it, every one becomes disguised, every one acts and appears willing; but nothing is true, nothing is real, nothing is sincere. Moral education is absent; violence is endured with impatience, and in the endurance it becomes hated, and it is actually hateful; and then what becomes of authority and respect? Fénelon had so much profound, so much delicate caution for the liberty as well as the dignity of nature in children, he wished not only that force should not be used with them, but even that their reasons should be discussed, that they should be induced to speak of the requirements of their education, in order to test their discernment, and give them a taste for what they should perform. And is it not, indeed, manifest that what they do without taste and against their will, that which they do by compulsion, benefits them not, and most frequently, like what they are forced to eat without hunger, injures and disgusts them. It is only what they accept lovingly, what enters naturally into their minds and hearts, that really nourishes their souls, that is converted into their own substance, and, if I may venture to say it, which becomes their mind and heart. The real aim of moral education is only that of persuading minds and hearts, and of bringing them up with a sincere love of virtue. How can we hope to accomplish this by material force, by servile fear, by imperious authority? No; if we wish to render children reasonable, it is necessary to speak reasonably to them, and they will listen; if we wish to render them virtuous, it is necessary to treat them with confidence; they are moved by it, and become grateful and cheerful. Fénelon went so far as to say that cheerfulness and confidence should be their ordinary disposition. A mind controlled by fear is always a weak mind; fear only cramps education, and consequently renders it superficial. The greater number of children who are brought up in this manner, have, when their education seems completed, to begin it again. After ten years, nothing has been done for them. People are sometimes terrified by lively and turbulent children; as for me, they never inspired me with fear: I was much more afraid of those whom I called sleeping waters. After the experiences of which I have spoken in the chapter on spoiled children, what I am about to say may appear less surprising. The truth is, I did not like children who had never rebelled against me; it was the former who gave me uneasiness; it was for them I dreaded the uncertainties of the future, and the awakening of the still slumbering passions. What a fault it is not to be able to endure anything from children! Fénelon formerly said, with real warmth of temper, to those parents and impatient teachers who were always reprimanding their pupils for making too much noise, "Permit a child to play." Do you not understand that his age requires, above all, noise, space, sun, movement? It is sufficient to see them, in order to comprehend it; it is their nature, it is their life. Give them, then, a large playground, gardens, walks; otherwise you put them to the torture. Remove walls and barriers; it is in the country, in the midst of fields and verdure, that children ought to be brought up. Is it not surprising that they can be induced to labor and remain immovable for ten or twelve hours each day? Do not refuse them liberty, at least during their recreation. Look at them then; it gives one pleasure to see them; for it is liberty itself, the most amiable, and also the most innocent form of it. They are content, provided they have change of place; let them have it. Fénelon pleasantly said, "A shuttlecock or a ball is sufficient;" at present it is a ball or a hoop. Guard well, then, against restraining them in their plays; guard against interdicting noisy recreations. These are what they love best, the diversions by which the body is called into full activity. Love them as they do. Their bodies will one day be less disposed to move; in the meanwhile take them as they are, or do not charge yourself with their education; for what can they do except impatiently endure your restraint, and rush eagerly to their plays while they can?[1] As for me, I asked one favor only from our children; that was, not to utter wild yells; again, when the weather and their temper seemed gloomy, I had toleration for them, and reserved my admonitions until some days after, when they had forgotten it.

Without doubt we may, and sometimes ought to, restrain children in their plays. Again, we may sometimes direct them, prompt them; but that is always a very delicate matter. To give one's self trouble about their plays is almost always lost trouble; they themselves invent enough of them; it is sufficient to permit them to do so; we should at most only make overtures to them: but let them always feel that they are free; it is what they require, it is their right. To wish to force them, to determine their taste on this head, in fine, to desire, even through kindness, that they should play more, to make them play in this way, is to continue the class during recreation; it is not understanding that recreation is the legitimate relaxation from the

[1] Fénelon.

class; that this liberty of a moment is the just, the necessary, indemnification for so long a constraint; it is exposing one's self to hear the most turbulent among them come up with a respectful simplicity, and say, what I heard once, and have never forgotten, "M. le Superieur, if you knew how amusing ourselves like that wearies us!" This pert little fellow was quite right. Ah! how differently the immortal friend of youth, whose authority and words I love so much to quote, thought! He not only wished that children should be permitted to play freely during their hours of recreation, but he went so far as to desire for young children "that study be hidden under the appearance of liberty and pleasure. Mix instruction with amusement; let wisdom show herself to them but at intervals, and with a smiling face; guard against fatiguing them by indiscreet exactitude." Again he said, "Let us suffer children sometimes to interrupt study by little diverting sallies. They require these distractions in order to relax their minds. Free curiosity stimulates their minds more than constraint. Permit their eyes to wander a little; for a child to see is to live. We should even permit them from time to time some digression or some play, so that their minds may be set at large; then let us gently lead them back to the task; too exact a regularity, in order to require from them uninterrupted studies, injures them much. Those who govern them often affect this regularity because, in order to profit by every moment, it suits them better than continual subjection."

One of the most serious, the most frequent, inconveniences of contrained education, is that of casting children into dejection, sometimes into despair, of breaking in them the most powerful springs of wisdom and virtue. Their minds become obscured, their courage disheartened; if they be lively, they become irritable; if they be dull, it renders them stupid.[1] Without doubt, there are natures that must be controlled by fear; but it must then be used as violent remedies are in the extremity of illness; for we always run the risk of impairing the constitution and wearing out the organs. I dwell on this point, because nothing is more difficult than to convince young teachers, especially young professors, of it. However, all the most eminent men are unanimous respecting this. A philosopher said, "Children should be induced to love goodness by gentleness and persuasion, never by harsh and humiliating punishments; such ill-treatment disheartens and repels them." Quintilian, also, has admirably expressed himself on the danger of intellectual or moral constraint in education: "Nothing dejects the minds of children so much as having a master who is too severe and too difficult to please; they become fretted and despairing; they look on everything with hatred; fear, which never leaves them, prevents them from making any effort. We should imitate the vine-dressers, who spare the vine while it is young; they are careful in pruning it then, for they know it fears the steel, and that it may suffer from the least wound. I am not so ill-instructed on the ability and inclinations of every age as to wish that a child be

[1] Fénelon.

severely pressed, and perfection in his work be required of him all at once; it is necessary to be careful especially of making him hate the sciences during the period when he should still love them, lest he be disgusted forever by the bitterness which at one time they caused him to feel."[1] This was Seneca's idea also. Is it just to rule children with as much strength and harshness as those animals deprived of reason? An experienced groom never startles his horse by redoubling his blows; it becomes skittish and restive if it do not occasionally feel a caressing hand. In the same manner, a sensible teacher does not unceasingly threaten his pupils; servile fear blunts their courage, extinguishes their ardor. But there is a much greater danger in moral constraint; it is that of making them hypocrites. Children are naturally timid and full of false shame; it is true, they are also naturally simple and open-hearted; but restrain them ever so little, or give them cause to fear you, and they become constrained, and never recover their early simplicity. The means of preventing so great an evil is, to accustom them to speak openly of their inclinations regarding all law-

[1] Ne illud quidem quod admoneamus indignum est, ingenia puerorum nimia interim emendationis severitate deficere; *nam et desperant et dolent, et novissime oderunt, et quod maxime nocet,* dum omnia timent, *nihil conantur. Quod etiam rusticis notum est, qui frondibus teneris non putant adhibendam esse falcem, quia reformidare ferrum videntur, et cicatricem nondum pati posse.* (Quintilian, vol. i. p. 245.) Nec sum adeo ætatum imprudens, ut instandum teneris protinus acerbe putem, exigendamque plenam operam. Nam id in primis cavere oportebit, ne studia, qui amare nondum potest, oderit, et amaritudinem semel perceptam etiam ultra rudes annos reformidet. (Quintilian, vol. i. p. 34.)

ful subjects; in order to do that, they must be allowed great liberty in expressing their thoughts and laying open their souls; otherwise this early artlessness of the natural emotions, which is so precious, becomes stifled in them. If they be never left free to evince their weariness, if they be always in subjection, if they be forced to like certain dull people or certain tedious books which displease them, if they be represented harshly, while they are displaying what they naturally are, everything soon becomes for them a source of dissimulation and a motive for disguise. They become politic, dissembling, indifferent to goodness, and secretly inclined to evil: in vain do they appear more docile than other children of the same age; they are no better. What do I say? You have taught them to outwardly repress all their inclinations. What comes to pass? All their bad habits, all their defects, increase, and ripen in silence. Their flexibility conceals a rebellious will; their deceitful disposition veils them from every eye; you never see them in their natural state, never know what they are at heart; and, in fine, their evil nature does not fully display itself until it is too late to set it right. It was the fear of all these disastrous results that caused Fénelon formerly to say, "Never put on, without extreme necessity, an austere and imperious air which makes children tremble. You close their hearts and repel their confidence, without which no fruit can be expected from education. Bring yourself to love them; let them be free with you, and do not fear allowing yourself to see their defects. In order to succeed in it, be indulgent to those who do not disguise themselves before you. Do not appear either astonished or irritated by their evil inclinations; on the contrary, compassionate their weakness. Sometimes the inconvenience, that they will be less restrained by fear, arises; but, on the whole, confidence and sincerity are more beneficial than rigorous authority. Besides, authority will not be permitted to find its place, if confidence and persuasion be not sufficiently great; it is necessary to begin always with an open-hearted, gay, and familiar manner."

But, I may be asked, must firmness never be made use of in education? Certainly I am very far from thinking or desiring anything of the kind. I have already said, education is a task of firmness. I do not know a human task which requires more of it, and on a future occasion I shall speak of this great and indispensable quality in the teacher. For the present, I say that firmness is not violence. I do not know of anything more firm than that which is gentle, nor of anything more weak than that which is violent. But it is especially when conscience is in question that children must be persuaded and induced to desire goodness, so that they desire it freely and independently of constraint. It is especially when faith, religion, and piety are in question, that it is necessary to be guarded from using compulsion towards them. Fénelon eloquently says, "No human power can break through the impenetrable intrenchment of liberty in a soul." And be not deceived, a soul of twelve years has in this way a power of incredible resistance. Constraint will for them convert faith into a false tongue, piety into odious formality, religion into a yoke of overwhelming hypocrisy. We shall only succeed in making them despise it if we oblige them to play there the part of a lying character, in which it is more important than elsewhere that moral liberty should act in all its plenitude. No, it is necessary that children spontaneously find religion to be beautiful, amiable, august. In vain have you worked if they have a sad and gloomy idea of it, if piety and virtue appear to them under the frightful image of violence, whilst irregularity presents itself to them under a pleasing aspect and with appearances of liberty. All is ruined; you have labored in vain. Why does religion present itself to the immense majority of children coming out of establishments for public instruction as cold, harsh, stupid, blighting? It is because it has never been anything else for them; because nothing has ever been done to give them any other idea of it; it is because, thanks to official constraint, they have never had anything free, anything generous, anything spontaneous, in their hearts; no real piety, no faith. Ah! without doubt, I do not desire, that, under pretext of respecting moral and religious liberty in youth, it should be thrown into indifference and scepticism. This extreme excites horror. It is sufficient to point it out in order to denounce it; but neither do I wish, that, under pretext of giving them a religious and moral education, religion should become an outward form, faith an imposed study, piety a habit of hypocrisy, hence a horrible scandal. Whosoever you may be, priest or laic, teacher or father of a family, if in the religious and moral education of children you know only how to command, to constrain, to make the evangelical and moral law be observed to the letter, you know nothing. You do not understand the first principles of educating souls; you have not the chief idea of this great work. When God and religion, man and his conscience, are in question, to strike, to reprehend, to correct, is nothing; it is necessary to cause them to be loved; but take care, in order to do that, you must love them yourself.

Permit me to ask you how you are in this respect. Without any doubt, if you wish to make a display of religion; if it suffice for you to reduce these poor children to the exact performance of certain external actions, beat the drum or toll the bell, every one rises up, every one marches; if you wish it, even if you have the determination, and they know it, every one trembles; you are obeyed; and I see all the classes in your establishment advance towards the chapel, all your pupils keeping step, in close ranks, in regular squadrons, under the guidance of their masters of study. I will quote the Archbishop of Cambrai to you: "There is an admirable police; and I desire a sincere religion." Where is it? What have you done for it? The more you wear out these children with a cold and imperious constraint, in order to make them outwardly fulfil their religious duties, so that official inspection may never find them defaulters, the more you compel them to put on a masked and hypocritical religion. Is this what you would wish? Who could say it? Who would venture to believe it? As for me, I never believed it. And then, when this odious constraint has been endured for ten years; when this child, thus placed between a chaplain who preaches and hears confessions, professors who have no belief, and the principal of an establishment who imperiously obliges every one to progress; when this child becomes a young man — from his fifteenth to his twentieth year — a wound, festering with hatred and irreligion, is being secretly formed in the bottom of his heart; he begins to suspect that an odious comedy has been played to him,[1] and sometimes twenty years are necessary in order to revive in that desolate soul a spark of religious belief, a breath of love and life. Certainly, those matters I have pointed out here are indescribable misfortunes; and, nevertheless, I have not yet depicted all. What if, at the same time that an outward constraint compels him to be religious, there be an interior constraint, a constraint in the depth of the soul, forcing him not to be so? If he be at the same time, as it were, forced not to believe, and, nevertheless, obliged to act always as if he believed; if there be educational establishments[2] where the observances of religion are publicly fulfilled, and privately devoted to contempt; where compulsion is exercised in favor of incredulity and vice; where bitter raillery pursues artless and pure virtue; where childhood cannot love God without becoming the object of the most insulting banter; where he must

[1] M. de Lamartine.

[2] I do not apply this name; such houses do not merit such a name; but I do not wish to indicate any thing or any one.

every day hear faith treated as superstition, piety as hypocrisy, and religion as fanaticism ; where he cannot pray sincerely and collectedly without being exposed to the basest treatment; if there be educational establishments where poor children must hide themselves in order to receive their God; where even the day of their first Communion they must try to escape from the looks and the derision of their older companions; if masters themselves be met with giving odious names to the most touching evidences of lively faith, to the last remnants of the sincere piety carried from home; if there be educational establishments where evil morals are, as it were, a necesity, and where innocence is inevitably shipwrecked; where the source of the evil is not only in the pupils, but in the domestics and the inspectors; where abuses become propagated, not alone by example and seduction, but are forced upon them, sometimes even by violence and threats,[1] — if all that be true; and if there be, at the same time, a country where Christian parents, where fathers and mothers of families, can be induced by constraint or indifference to place their children in these houses, in order to prepare them for the examinations necessary for any profession or a career; and if in these same houses, besides this frightful immorality and irreligion, youth be condemned, at the same time, to submit to the most

[1] We know this is what M. Lallemand, Professor of the Faculty of Medicine at Montpellier, and invested with this title by the Council of Public Instruction, who had chosen him on account of their confidence in him, reveals, as the results of his most attentive observations on the subject.

fatal intellectual constraint that ever existed, under masters who have not time to care, or even to know, the greater number of their pupils; if it be the destiny of many of these poor children to vegetate thus under the weight of hopeless weariness, in stupidity of mind, in continued debasement of character, in annihilation of heart, detesting these accursed places as one detests a prison, and having no longer life or soul but to sigh for the day of enfranchisement; and if, on coming out from thence, and before presenting themselves to enter any liberal career, these young people should meet with an examination to be undergone, such as would cause a miserable failure to the greater number among them, and reduce them afterwards to fall back on themselves with all the weight of their disappointed future and their blighted youth; if entire generations be thus devoted by this deplorable rule, I would ask, what nation is sufficiently unfortunate to be obliged to submit to so strange a social tyranny? I would ask, what youth is this, devoted to an intellectual and moral slavery so disastrous? I would ask if there be not some oppressed conscience courageous enough to send forth a cry of sorrow? I would ask what this nation has done in order to be judged unworthy of the noblest of liberties, — the liberty of the soul? I would ask the name of this nation: what is its faith, its credibility, its place in the orbit of truth and justice in this world? I would ask what hidden, mysterious, frightful power weighs on its destiny? I would ask everything; I would ask if this nation has been one day cursed? If it should always be so? I would ask if these fathers of families have sworn never to be fathers? if these mothers have forgotten the rights and sacred duties of maternal authority? And if at length I should be told, This is the great, the generous French nation; well, I would hide my face in my hands, and I would say with the philosopher, *Ætas parentum, pejor avis, tulit nos nequiores, mox daturos progeniem vitiosiorem.*

CHAPTER XX.

OF THE CHILD, AND THE RESPECT DUE TO THE LIBERTY OF HIS VOCATION.

No one is placed on earth in order to do nothing; there is a state, an office, a labor, for each. I cannot conclude what I ought to say regarding the child, and the respect due to the liberty of his nature, without treating of a question which is in this place the most serious and most decisive, which is to be found at the bottom of all others, and the solution of which appears to me indispensable for the perfect enlightenment of the difficulties that we have up to the present been examining. I wish to speak on the great question of a vocation, and of the choice of a state for each. Be it understood that this question concerns, in the highest degree, the liberty of the child, his happiness in this world and the next. It also touches on the greatest interests of the family and social order. In speaking of it, I will say everything that I consider necessary. At the same time, I will not allow myself to be drawn into an infinity of details; but I shall lay down at least the general and incontestable principles of the matter. There are three positive truths. First, no one is placed on earth in order to do nothing; there is, then, a labor, a rule of duties, a state, for each. Second, nothing on earth happens by chance. Providence governs everything here, the most trifling events, and, with much more reason, the greatest; there is, then, for each and every state a vocation from God. Third, education should prepare every one for his state, his vocation; this is the consequence of that which precedes.

FIRSTLY — NO ONE IS PLACED ON EARTH IN ORDER TO DO NOTHING. I ask of my readers the desire of following me strictly in all the grave and profound considerations which I ought to bring under their notice. It is here, especially, I have need to appeal to their most serious and re-collected attention. The matters I have to speak of will be at times very delicate, perhaps even painful. I will speak of them with caution; but, however, with the simplicity and frankness which my conscience, the great concerns I treat of, and even my respectful devotion for those of whom I am about to speak, command. There are different kinds of parents, who determine, with singular sincerity, not to require their sons to do anything in this world; and who, in order to justify themselves, bring forward motives or excuses, reasons or errors, of different natures. I have met with some, very virtuous, who, having a horror of the corrupt society of the present age, said, "All states are perilous. In such times, the only matter to be looked to is his salvation. Since our children are condemned to pass through this sad world, they shall avoid, at least as far as possible, the contagion of it." It is true, this class of parents is not very numerous. I have seen others who said, "I cannot allow my sons to take part in passing events; my political opinions are opposed to them, my honor, the honor of my family, does not permit me to do it." These latter were most frequently to be met with some years ago; the circumstances which dictated this language to them have changed. In fine, I have seen a much greater number of fathers of families who considered they found in their wealth sufficient reason for exempting their sons from all serious labor, and leaving them without any occupation on earth. It is to these I shall first reply. When parents in this category came to confide their sons to me, and I said to them, "What shall he one day have to do, and what do you intend him to be?" some of them appeared offended. The most benevolent were good-naturedly surprised; and all seemed to tell me, You do not know us; we are not what you think. Each actually said to me, "But my son does not want anything. His future is certain. I have labored for him. He will enjoy my wealth, without being obliged to labor in his turn." To all that, I had, and at present still have, but one answer to make; it is the words of the ancient philosopher: *Homo nascitur ad laborem, sicut avis ad volatum* (Job, v. 7) — "Man is born to labor as the bird is to fly;" so that living without laboring is not only living outside the conditions of human nature, it is extinguishing, it is stifling, it is annihilating life in one's self; it is not living. Be not deceived on this point. The words of Job, in their simplicity, conceal a very profound meaning. Yes, man is born to labor; that is to say, for action, for life; for he lives

— is somebody — only by what he does. Whosoever does nothing, is nothing, and never will be anything. Observe well; I am not going to speak here of the sweetness of labor, and the happiness it confers on those who love it; I am not going to speak of the protection it affords to virtue, and how it guards it; I will not even speak of the influence labor has on the character, and what strength it communicates to it. I wish to speak only of one view respecting it; which is, that labor is the necessary condition of life for every man coming into this world. It is essentially his vocation; rich or poor, he ought to fulfil it. Those who are not poor, and do not consider it necessary to work in order to gain their living laboriously, do not understand sufficiently how they need it, in order to preserve, to ennoble, to elevate, the life which they received from God. Liberty is much spoken of at present; I have spoken of it myself; but the law of liberty is the law of labor. Liberty, activity, labor, are matters closely allied. For this reason, frivolous or idle people are not made for liberty. What I should especially call attention to is, that labor is the great law of creation. God, in creating the world, in giving us life, has performed a noble and divine work; and we ourselves ought to labor in order to live; that is to say, in order to preserve, to develop, to elevate, the life God has given us. Look at all the great faculties of the soul; what are they? Active powers, which require labor. To condemn them to inertness, to deny them this generous activity, which essentially distinguishes them from matter, is to disparage, to degrade, to annihilate them. The corporal faculties themselves cannot be preserved or developed but by exercise; that is to say, by labor. All the physical, intellectual, and moral powers of man, which grow and increase according as man uses them energetically, droop and run to waste when they are allowed to pine in idleness; in a word, whosoever does nothing in this world, by that same does wrong; he becomes depraved, he destroys himself; and this is one of the meanings of the well-known saying, taken from the Holy Scriptures: "Idleness teaches every evil" — *Omnem malitiam docuit otiositas.* Bossuet fearlessly gave these forcible instructions to the son of Louis XIV. I have often admired how energetically this holy bishop exerted himself to make severe truths penetrate the mind and heart of that young prince. "It is not without some benefit," said he to him, "and in order that you should not make use of them, that God has given you intelligence and all those noble faculties which enlighten you, and aid you to recall the past, to know the present, to foresee the future. Whosoever does not deign to profit by the gifts of heaven, necessarily makes enemies of God and men. For it must not be expected that men will respect him who despises that which makes him man, or that God protects him who makes no account of his most excellent gifts." In continuation, Bossuet announces to his pupil, that all the faculties of his intellect will soon be annihilated, if they be not cultivated by labor: "Do not commence in inattention and idleness a life which ought to be so occupied and active. The consequence of so beginning will be, that, being born with much genius, you can only impute to yourself the extinction or inutility of this admirable light, which is bestowed upon you as a rich gift from God. Of what use are well-made weapons if you never take them in your hands? So, likewise, of what benefit is genius if you do not apply it? It is so much loss. And as it is with dancing and writing, if you give them up, you come, through want of habit, to forget both; so also, if you do not exercise your mind, it becomes torpid, it falls into a kind of lethargy; and, whatever efforts you may afterwards desire to make in order to shake it off, will be too late. Shameful passions will spring up in you; love of pleasure and passion will incite you to all sorts of crimes; and, the light which alone could have guided you being once extinguished, you will be placed beyond counting on any assistance." It is, then, true that education should not maintain that nothing is to be done, and even hinder anything from being done. It is, then, true that all on earth, rich or poor, are called upon to do something — have a labor, a vocation, to fulfil on earth. It is, then, true, whatever may be said of man's inclination to idleness, and whatever the natural indolence of his character and mind may be, that labor and activity are an essential condition of his life, and a requirement of his nature. "By an admirable economy, every creature pleases himself in using his powers; the soul delights in the play of its faculties, it enjoys it as much as it can; so that its true repose is to be found even in labor."[1]

[1] M. Ozanam.

It was not alone after man had become guilty and sinful that labor was imposed upon him as a law; during his happy sojourn in the ancient Eden, innocent man was obliged to labor: *Posuit eum in Paradiso voluptatis, ut operaretur eum* (Genesis). Labor was one of the conditions of his happiness, of his dignity, of his existence. It is true, labor, which ought to be but the charm and ornament of his life, soon became a part of his punishment; this formidable decree, which still pursues the most remote of his posterity, was soon pronounced against him, "Thou shalt eat thy bread in the sweat of thy brow" —*In sudore vultus tui vesceris pane* (Genesis). "But a merciful Will soon also causes the chastisement to repair in a manner the fault, and man, in courageously submitting to the humiliation, finds another source of greatness. By fructifying the earth with his sweat, as the sun fertilizes it with his heat, and the clouds with their rain, he enters into the regular order of the universe. God employs him, and consequently rehabilitates him; as soon as he becomes useful, his merit begins. Here is the Christian dogma of labor, the profound meaning of which is no longer understood."[1] Certainly, after such strong, such noble reasons, after such religious motives, I have the right to say to those to whom I am at present expounding my ideas, You wish to be something in this world; you wish to live, and do nothing. Well, all moral and social laws, all natural laws, are opposed to this. Idleness is the inevitable ruin of

[1] M. Ozanam.

all the faculties. These faculties are essentially active; they require perpetual culture, development, that is to say, labor, or else they will remain in or fall into fallow. The Scripture says, they produce but troubles and thorns: *spinas ac tribulos.* Bitter fruits, wild fruits; indeed, the only fruits they can produce while they remain uncultivated. You wish to be something in this world, and to do nothing; but this is really an absolute impossibility; you would do wrong. And, moreover, doing nothing in this world is foolishly desiring to escape the great law of human nature, which is for man not only the law of his preservation, his improvement, and his life, but which is for him, since the original fall, at the same time the law of expiation and regeneration. And by what right do you desire that this universal law, this sentence, which commands you to fill up all the days that separate your birth from your death with a noble and religious labor, should not be accomplished for you or your children? You are rich; this excuse, instead of justifying you, renders your idleness more culpable. I will say to you, with a holy and eloquent bishop, whose name remains dear to Christian youth,[1] "If you have been paid beforehand, is that a reason you should not earn your salary?" We now come to those who pretend that the times are so evil, and that their children have nothing to do but seek their salvation. I will say that such subterfuges and such strange subtleties are unworthy of their sense and their faith. Without

[1] M. Borderies, Bishop of Versailles.

doubt, it is necessary that this child should seek his salvation, and it is his great business in this world. But if it be true that without labor there can be no salvation, and that idleness can be nothing less than a revolt against Providence; if it be a divine institution that the faculties imparted to man ought to be cultivated and developed by labor; if experience demonstrates, moreover, that these faculties cannot be left inactive without danger to virtue; in fine, if it be written that God ought, according to the words of the Gospel, cast into exterior darkness those who have done nothing on earth; if He does not wish to count among His servants the unprofitable servants, what reply will you have to make at the judgment of God, who will demand of you an account of that talent which He had confided to you, of the soul of your son, of the uselessness and loss of his life? Besides, I ought to add, labor is not only the law of nature, morality, and religion, for the individual man; it is also the law of society for the human species.

No one on earth has been created in order to do nothing; but every one has been created in order to be useful to his kind. Egotism can neither be the law of domestic society, which means the Family, nor the law of temporal society, which means the State, nor of the great spiritual society called the Church. It is the duty of every one to labor for himself, but it is his duty also to assist his fellow-creature; and he who buries his life in idleness adds to the wrong which he does himself that of culpable inhumanity to his brother-man. What! every thing around you is in activity, every thing stirring, every thing moving, every one laboring; and, in the midst of this universal movement, you alone remain idle, sinfully unprofitable, in a shameful repose! You seem to count as nothing the troubles and sweat of your fellow-creatures. Their fatigues and their labors are for you but a spectacle which appears to amuse your leisure; or, rather, you establish yourself as the immovable centre of all this motion, and you reap the benefit of it without relinquishing your inaction; without dreaming of offering, in your turn, any services to your fellow-creatures in exchange for their labors. Labor is due to your parents, to your children, to your family, to your country; it is idleness that allows the patrimony of wealth or of honor, which they had received from their fathers, to slip from the hands of so many unworthy heirs; it is idleness, which, like a gnawing worm, silently undermines, and at length demolishes, fortunes apparently established on the most solid foundations, and prepares distress and contempt as sole heritage for the sons of a wealthy and respected father. And hence it is, that, in great nations, so many noble families decay, so many noble names die out. Hence those illustrious families become degraded, and sometimes disgraced; incapable of understanding any thing, of governing any thing, establishing any thing, of perpetuating any thing, and, in the hour of public danger, of saving any thing. Hence those ancient celebrities gradually become enveloped in obscurity, and miserably disappear; and I do not hesitate to proclaim that it is, beyond dispute, one of the most terrible maledictions which can fall upon a nation. Woe to the nation whose great races become degraded and die out! I am conscious I shock more than one prejudice here, and my language may appear bitter; therefore I wish to give my idea some development in order to explain it; I touch on the most delicate, and I believe also the most important, part of my subject. I will, at first, say without circumlocution, and without any regard for the prejudices of the times, I apply the words great family, great race, great name, to those families, those races, those names, which have become historical on account of signal services rendered to their country, at whatever period it may be; who have acquired their celebrity by fame of arms in the field, their skill in eminent negotiations and in the management of political affairs, by brilliant talent, and sometimes genius, in science and literature; in fine, by sanctity of morals and greatness of character in the magistracy or the church. It is being descended from those races which constitutes what, in the French tongue, is called birth, of which M. Royer Collard said, "An illustrious birth will be always a greatness, and respect for past glory has its source in noble sentiments." The authority of this grave publicist on this point cannot be questioned. I will again add to the unquestionable and undisputed titles which constitute great families ownership of the soil or territorial wealth, to the degree in which it becomes a social power. Here are what I call the great families, the great races, of a country. Well, I acknowledge without evasion, I love those great families; I respect, I venerate them, because I love, I respect, I venerate great memories and great deeds. I do not know any nation whose power and glory they may be, and which has not a natural tendency to look to them for its chiefs, its warriors, its ministers, its principal magistrates, its administrators. This may, perhaps, be a prejudice, but it is a profound one; and save in troubled times, when this prejudice sometimes becomes converted into hate, it is always returned to. In republics, as well as in monarchies, among ancient as well as modern nations, the eyes of the people, in the midst of their wants or public disasters, naturally turn themselves towards those illustrious families, and it is among them they always hope to find more surely, more abounding, the knowledge of human affairs, the wisdom of political life, the experience, the devotion, the power, the authority, which alone can govern, defend, or save, a country. I do not hesitate to affirm that in no place has this prejudice, if it be one, deeper root, nor does it exercise a more irresistible power, than in France. They who think that revolutions are excited amongst us in order to put an end to titles and pride of birth, strangely deceive themselves; revolutions are excited amongst us rather in order to take possession of them; every one wishes to enjoy them in his turn, or at least replace them on the scene. It is also a curious fact, worthy of being observed, revolutions in our country have only multiplied titles and vanities of this kind. However that may be, an intelligent nation will always honor sentiments of hereditary dignity, which, though engendering vanity in some, is not the less eminently rational and useful in itself. In France, brilliant merit which rises from obscurity will always find its newly-acquired fame sanctioned by some new title; it must also be said, that, in spite of democratic progress, ambitious vanity will always seek to clothe itself with borrowed splendor; and this contagion spreads in such a manner, that there will soon be no longer a village in our country that will not have hidden with its name the obscure name hitherto borne by an unknown celebrity. Without doubt, in this place, it is the abuse of right, but right is forcibly outliving it; it is reasonable and natural, and superior to all those doubtful celebrities, superior to all those equivocal names. There will always be great names, great races, illustrious families, and also the people will always love them; as M. de Chateaubriand wrote: "The people will always regret the tombs of some of the sires De Montmorency, on which it comforted them to kneel during Mass."[1] And M. de Chateaubriand himself will, in spite of the foibles of his life, and in spite of the surprise and the regret which the "Memoirs from his Tomb" caused to his admirers, leave behind as illustrious a name; perhaps his tomb will also have its pilgrims; and if I happened to say to the young heir of his blood, or to that of one of the heroic celebrities of the empire, for example, the Duke de Montebello, that the name they bear is nothing, neither one nor the other would believe me, and they would be right; no more would the people believe me. The rigidness with which

1 "Genius of Christianity."

they require great virtues from great names, is it not in itself a just, but unexceptional, evidence of the natural and instinctive homage which opinion renders to them? Without doubt, a great name is an inheritance for a family; and a distinguished man, in giving lustre of birth to his sons, also imposes on them the obligation of his virtues; for, according to an axiom of honor, entirely French, *noblesse oblige.* But a great name, a great man, is also the glory of a nation; he is the glory of humanity itself; for this profound reason, that it is a name, that he is a man, in whom Providence has caused its gifts to shine forth, and from whom all claim their share of this honor conferred on human nature. Here is the reason that national instinct will always honor glorious names and great races. If this prejudice has remained so powerful in France, it is, perhaps, because no nation was more rich in truly great names, in real celebrities. The old French nobility owes its ancient honor and imperishable glory to the sacrifice of life that it has heroically made during fourteen centuries. Since Clovis, the Frank race has not ceased to shed its blood on all the battle-fields of Asia, Africa, and Europe, for the cause of God, the poor, and the country. The new nobility has also gloriously conquered, and paid with its blood for its escutcheons, though it should still have need of a tradition sustained by worthy heirs, and confirmed by time.

Now, then, to come down again from these high and general considerations to the practical subject which I treat of, I will, without hesitation, say to the sons of great names, to the heirs of great races, Among a brilliant, generous nation, where glory will always be a passion, and historical memories a greatness, as long as you will be worthy of your great names, you will be in the first rank; whatever those beneath you may say against you, you will have the first place. The nation itself will give it to you. Merit always being equal, it is you who will carry it away; and if individual justice seems hurt by this preference, there is a higher justice, national justice, which must be satisfied. Yes, a great name, supported by a great education, will always have success in France; and I am happy in saying, to the honor of our times, model nobles are not wanting to us in this respect, even among our young contemporaries. But to do nothing in the midst of this immense bustle of all classes, which tends to ameliorate, to ennoble, to elevate, to enrich them, by industry, by commerce, by agriculture, by the labors of political life; doing nothing is abdicating, is annihilating one's self. Not to understand that we live in times when it is necessary to make the wealth we have received from our ancestors pardonable; to authorize the new-comers of modern society to say that the descendants of great families remain, in the midst of universal progress, unshaken in their prejudices of race, stationary in their wealth, retrograding in their ideas; that they do nothing, and do not wish to do anything, — it is impossible. And those of whom I speak — do they not see, that when luxury and idleness are united with division of property, and equality of inheritance, they diminish, become parcelled out, and devoured?

Alas! with many, every thing outside still glitters; every thing within is already wretchedness and ruin. Doing nothing, simply from a material point of view, is the annihilation of the only means by which they still retain for themselves some superiority and property. In former times, they had the glorious privilege of military service; they were the first in times of war to shed their blood for their country. Certainly that was something; they became great by it. If culture of the mind gained nothing, the character was strengthened by it. Generosity, heroic devotion, and all the warlike virtues which have made the French nation the first in Europe, displayed all their splendor in them. At present, matters are changed; the sword and valor are always prized amongst us; but every hand may aim to carry the sword. The command of armies is no longer a privilege; like the crown of Philip Augustus, it is to the most worthy. And besides, war is dying out; it seems to have obeyed the ancient motto, *cedant arma togæ;* it gives place to industry, commerce, politics, science, and the arts; it is to this side the future of Europe now appears to be tending, at least as far as the shortness of human foresight may venture to predict. Is it prejudice or reason that makes one disdainfully reject extensive commerce, great trade, frequently the magistracy itself, and the greater number of public careers? Is it just or wise not to consider any other employment, any other glory, suitable than that of arms? Genoa, Venice, Carthage, and Florence, those great queens of the sea, those illustrious rulers of the commerce of the East and the West, thought otherwise. Did not the Genoese, Venetian, and Florentine nobles elevate themselves by their alliances as high as the most ancient sovereign houses of Europe? Are not those examples, that experience, at least a forcible lesson, a decisive reply, to the heirs of those great families among us who condemn themselves to do nothing, and who, as a necessary consequence, become depraved, abiding without intelligence, without action, without influence? How many times have I not heard the most eminent men of the country sigh over the fate of those whose cause I am at present pleading! — for it is their cause I plead against themselves. What sensible man, what honorable woman, has not deplored the life of so many young people, who appear to have no desire but that of resigning the dignity of their birth, and, in fine, to make use of the too common, and, alas! too well-known expression, "Only know how to lounge about the pavement of Paris!" The pavement of Paris, that is to say, the Jockey Clubs, *Boulevard des Italiens*, unlimited play, the green-rooms of the theatres, horses, dogs, women, and many unmentionable dissipations. Here are the deplorable consequences of this sad affair, — nothing to do. But is not the fatal prejudice, that a real gentleman ought to do nothing, or at least can do nothing, absolutely the same prejudice that existed in former times, when esquires and lords maintained that they ought to know nothing, not even to read and write; that they were created only to wield the sword; and that science and literature suited but plebeians and the clergy? That prejudice, which had at least something energetic and proud in its primitive rudeness, has become more perpetuated than is supposed in French ideas, while losing its energy. Hence this fear of public education existed in former times, and still to some extent to-day; hence so many of the children of the nobility, save some rare and honorable exceptions, are condemned to private education, that is to say, too frequently to effeminacy of character and mediocrity of mind. I heard a man of great sense utter this remarkable speech: "A usurping and clever government, wishing to free itself from the great races, and outroot them from the country, can reduce them, through respect for themselves, to the exigency of bringing up their children in their homes in the circumscribed sphere of private education and a private tutor." I have no hesitation in believing this has always been the great danger of royal races and princely educations. Bossuet formerly expressed his ideas of it in these terms to the son of Louis XIV.: "What makes men of condition, if they be not seriously watchful, fall into idleness and a species of languor, is the abundance to which they are born. Want arouses other men, and anxiety for their fate unceasingly induces them to labor. Those who possess the wealth necessary, not only for living, but for pleasure and grandeur, persuade themselves they have nothing to gain by labor. But it must not be supposed that wisdom will come to you with the same facility, and without your laboring seriously to acquire it. It is not in our power to put into your mind what will serve to cultivate reason and virtue, while you will do nothing. It is necessary, then, you should stimulate and apply yourselves to labor, in order that reason should spring up in you. This ought to be your only occupation; you have only that to do and think of. Are you not too happy in having matters disposed in such a manner that other labors do not regard you, and that you have only to cultivate your mind and form your intellect?" Louis XIV., who had known, through his own experience, all the misfortunes of a neglected education, wished to spare his son and his grandson these dangers, and he himself drew up with admirable strictness the rule of labor for the grand Dauphin. Here is what Bossuet wrote to Pope Innocent XII. respecting it: "The law of study imposed by the king was not to allow any day to pass without studying. He considered there was a great difference between passing the whole day in idleness, and taking some diversion in order to relax the mind. It is necessary that a child should play and be merry, — that stimulates him; but he must not give himself up to play and pleasure in such a manner as not to recall to mind every day those most serious matters, the study of which would languish if they were too much interrupted. As the whole life of princes is occupied with, and none of their days exempt from, great cares, it is good to train them during childhood to apply themselves to whatever is most serious, and make them give some hours to it every day, in order that their minds may be trained to labor, and quite accustomed to serious subjects when they shall have to attend to public matters."

If I may, then, give some advice to those ancient families who still remain to France, I will say to them, Have no fear of what is a blessing from heaven, a numerous family; a number of sons are the wealth of their father, their name, and their family! Marry them well; give them wives of sound constitutions and sincere piety; make worthy marriages, fruitful and without stain, irreproachable alliances, from which will spring a pure and healthy race. Bring up your sons vigorously; give them a solid and brilliant education in everything, and afterwards push them forward in some career; and, even though the equality of shares shall leave but a moderate fortune to each of them, they will be great and wealthy by their education, by their labor, by their name, and even by their number. They will sustain and strengthen each other in the different posts to which Providence and the enlightened solicitude of their fathers shall have called them.

This is an observation which will not escape the attention of men, of minds which follow with a religious and Christian glance the ways of Providence: there is a visible, even a temporal, benediction for numerous families; and I have almost always seen realized in their favor those desires which they submit to God, with a noble dependence on His goodness, and which, among many others, are replaced by culpable, and, most frequently, impotent calculations. Among these numerous children, many at least will have distinguished talents; well brought up, they will become superior men; they will do honor to their brothers; they will sustain their name; they will enrich their family; they will govern, perhaps they will save, their country! Yes; God will bless them. Why do we so frequently see great names sink into oblivion, noble stocks waste away? It is because there is but one or two children to be found among them; an only son, perhaps, who, effeminately brought up, has dishonored his race.

I have spoken of spoiled children; it very rarely happens that there can be spoiled children in a large family. An only son or an only daughter is almost always idolized by the family, and the object of the most frivolous anxieties. There is no serious care, no elevated idea, in the education of these children, of whom they seek to make beings destined only for the ease and enjoyment of this world, certain of being wealthy, without ever doing anything, without ever laboring, without ever giving themselves the least trouble. How can they expect that the blessing of God will descend on these miserable educations, and also these pitiful calculations of wealth, these base and impious computations of a future, in which Providence is absolutely counted as nothing? Without doubt, it is necessary that the heads of families should have, inasmuch as they can, importance, through their wealth; and this is what our modern laws have forgotten too much. But numerous branches are also necessary to uphold, extend, and strengthen each other.

Permit me to repeat again to the heads of great families, If you know how to give your numerous sons a high intellectual education, they will always and everywhere be at the head of their fellow-citizens, first by valor, when it will be necessary. The field of battle will again find you what you have always been; your race will not fail. They will be first also by intellect; if you will it, you have the ability. The past verifies this. Witness Turenne and Condé, D'Anguesseau, Cardinal de Polignac, La Rochefoucauld, Fénelon, and so many others. Let trade progress; it is not destined to conquer the world; and, if it were, if you leave traders to aspire, as they do, only to an ordinary and professional education; if, in taking what is necessary from this inferior education, you know how to elevate yourself still more, to strengthen, ennoble, enlighten yourself by high education of the understanding,—you will still rule all; you will necessarily surpass, you will govern, you will direct commerce itself; you will save it from its abuse; you will elevate it even to yourself, and you will remain in your place, what you are, a Montmorency, a D'Harcourt, or any other of those renowned names which rule opinion by hereditary prestige. But if these glorious destinies surprise you, if they seem to you beyond our age, still I will not agree, even though resigning them for you, that you ought to do nothing on earth. I will never grant that you can be without any labor in this world. No; the chase, romances, horses, and dogs do not suffice for any thing and any one. I will say to you, with the Holy Scriptures, *Non oderis opera laboriosa, et rusticationem creatam ab altissimo*—"Do not despise labor, not even the tilling of the earth, agriculture, which was invented by the Almighty; agriculture is the foundation of human life." Yes; if trade and commerce do not suit you, be noble, and, if in your power, be distinguished agriculturists. That is still a beautiful and glorious phase of labor. Be faithful to the soil which has made your name and your fortune; the soil in its turn will be faithful to you, and the population will pray for you. If they be less inclined to wish you well during the past twenty-five years, it is because you have too much abandoned them. Why despise your true and solid greatness? Why linger in Paris, leading a life unworthy of you, in ruinous clubs of play and pleasure? Why throw the remainder of your wealth into those abysses of luxury, and all the misdemeanors that idleness leads to, rather than dwell honorably on your property; rather than strike those deep roots in the country which revolutions themselves have not been able to tear out; rather than make yourself loved and respected, by shedding benefits on the poor people around you, who only ask to render you freely that allegiance which they always maintained towards your ancestors? Why leave such noble cares to your men of business, your stewards, your notaries, your advisers, who make themselves loved and chosen instead of you, who really succeed you, and are to-day representing the people in your place? There is a saying of the Scriptures, the weight of which I pray God never to let fall on any one in my country; but if there ever was a terrible saying, it is one, and worthy of being meditated on by every one. Here it is: "The votaries of pleasure," says the Holy

Ghost, "will be eternally unprofitable"—*Auferetur factio lascivientium.*[1]

Let me conclude. Every one on earth has something to do, a path to follow, an end to attain, a labor to accomplish, a place to occupy; in a word, grave obligations, serious duties, to fulfil. Labor, which is the application of the mind, is also its power and its glory. Without labor, without application, nothing can be done, either in this world or the next. God and men despise, reject, as an unprofitable servant, the man who does nothing, who is not available for any thing. Application alone makes great men, great saints, heroes, and men of genius.

All that is rare to-day, because serious labor, profound application, is no longer understood. Poets, literary men, historians, philosophers, no longer apply themselves; and we know what the greater number of them have become during the last fifty years.

But, if the troubles of the times do not permit you to aspire to the management of public affairs, at least know how to apply yourself to the management of your property, your family, your servants, your children. Acquire the agricultural, industrial, even commercial knowledge, which the nature of your wealth, your revenues, require, and in order to mention by their names those matters necessary for your workshops, your mills, your lands, your cattle. Acquire, at least, all that is necessary for you, in order to turn them to good account. Rule your children especially, and their education; excellent work, to

[1] Amos.

which you should never be strangers. Regulate your servants, so frequently left to themselves. Direct good works; understand how to establish them generously, to propagate them zealously. Occupy yourself with the villagers who surround you; know how to make them love you; comfort the poor. Be in your parish and in your province a useful man, a charitable adviser. Improve everything around you, — bridges, roads, churches, schools, the parish edifices. Above all, reflect upon this last instruction; which is, Whatever may be the troubles of the times, no one can ever be permitted to sacrifice society, morality, or religion, to sacrifice himself and his children to the passing interests of politics, and to make revolutions a claim to doing nothing. Can it be possible that France has ever had statesmen who could see with indifference what becomes of opulent youth among us? Can it be possible that any experienced thinker would believe that the country could find its present and future well-being in steeple-chases, dandies, lions, and all the corrupt societies of young people, who give themselves up to them, and who seem to say to their country, It must no longer count on us? I cannot believe it; it would be too strange a blindness. No, no; idle youth, gilded youth, however brilliant it may be, is no advantage to a country, either in peace or war; neither society nor politicians, neither religion nor morality, neither the present nor the future, can be satisfied with it. There is, then, a place and duties marked out for every one in this world. What is this place? What are these duties? Who shall decide on the choice to be made? Shall it be chance, caprice, or compulsion? No; it shall be Providence; for nothing on earth happens by accident; nothing, in such a matter, can be given up to chance; for each person, for each state, there is a vocation from God. This is what remains for us to examine, in order to clear up the important question which occupies us.

CHAPTER XXI.

NOTHING ON EARTH HAPPENS BY ACCIDENT; THERE IS, THEN, FOR EVERY ONE, AND FOR EACH STATE, A VOCATION FROM GOD.

No; nothing on earth happens by accident. A hair does not fall from our heads but by the will of Heaven. With much greater reason, the employment of our noblest faculties, and the labor of our whole life, cannot be abandoned to the caprices of chance. Whosoever we may be, we ought, then, to study attentively the designs of God respecting us; we ought to seek religiously to know what God requires that we should do on earth; the place He wishes us to occupy in this world; that for which He destines us; in a word, to what He calls us.

Applying one's self to know this vocation, at least in general and with sufficient probability to satisfy an attentive and prudent judgment, is one of the greatest duties of parents with regard to their children; it is the foundation on which will rest the choice they shall have to make of the kind of education they will give them. It is, indeed, manifest that to know what a child can and ought to do in this world is the first condition requisite for deciding in what manner he must be prepared for it. But they will say to me, How is the vocation of a child to be known and to be studied? that must be singularly difficult. No; to do it at the suitable time, and with religious attention, alone is necessary; the indications of Providence are never wanting. We have somewhere said, education continues the work of creation. The first matter, then, to be known in education is, how the Creator wishes to be aided in the development of His work and His designs; for what end He has placed such a child on earth; to what He destines him: what method, what kind, of education suits best the end it should aim to attain, can then be decided on; the destiny there is question of his fulfilling; and for that the indications of Providence are more explicit than is commonly supposed. It is rare when certain general indications, very easily discerned, certain tastes, certain capacities, certain very marked dispositions, do not determine, at a sufficiently early age, the probable vocation of the child, and, consequently, the befitting education. Understand; I do not speak of early education; that ought to be nearly the same for all. I speak of that other education, which extends, whatever may be its form and its name, from ten to twenty years of age; and, without repeating in this place what influence the means which education has at its disposal ought to have on the child, it is sufficient for me to observe, it is at this age, especially, the young man perfects himself, and that his vocation is decided. The kind of studies to which he devotes himself, the time he bestows on them, the tastes they inspire in him, the application he brings to them, the success he obtains in them; the degree and extent to which his intellect attains; the first emotions, good or evil, which the passions cause him to display; the features of character more or less delineated; and, in fine, the influence, more or less strong, of grace; the supernatural inclinations which it sometimes gives for certain more perfect vocations, — these are the means of studying and knowing to what God calls him, what God requires that he should do on earth. At the same time, I do not desire nor ought I to exaggerate anything here. The choice of a state has almost always sufficiently great latitude; there are different vocations more or less perfect. The masters of ethics acknowledge that if there be, among these vocations, some at times more arbitrary, from which one cannot withdraw himself, except at the risk of imperilling everything in his life, there are others more independent, among which hesitation is permissible, even proper. The reason of it is very simple. How many professions are there, among which the differences are so trifling a matter, that preferring one to the other is manifestly without appreciable importance!

I do not expect, then, that the vocation can be determined with rigorous precision, even to its most trifling details; but what I maintain is, that, at least, the kind of vocation is usually indicated by means easily recognized, and that error would be full of danger. For example, living in the world or living out of the world; the religious state or the married state; here are vocations and states entirely different from each other. And even in the numerous worldly states, there are some of them totally unlike; for instance, the gown or the sword, agriculture or trade, the navy or civil service, the career of literature, sciences, or arts. These various careers require such different capacities, that choosing blindly or by chance for a young man, among professions which resemble each other so little, would be manifestly to overshadow, to overcast, to paralyze, his whole life; it would be binding him to a life for which, perhaps, he was never intended, and in which success and happiness would be morally impossible for him. Hence, as the differences between the principal kinds of vocation are strongly marked, it is easy to avoid error, little trouble as one may wish to take, by studying, with the double assistance of attention and time, the differences which are to be met with among the physical, intellectual, moral, and religious dispositions of the various children.

The supernatural influence, if he aspire to the supernatural and more perfect vocations, and whatever be the vocation he aspires to, the capacity which renders him fit for such or such profession; the want of capacity which removes him from it; the inclination and taste which facilitate the study and success of it; the evil dispositions, the deficiencies, the passions, that would find in such a state fatal nourishment, which must be denied them; the good dispositions, the virtues, which find in such another state the happy, fruitful support which must be afforded them; in fine, assuming and wisely considering all the rest, the circumstances of birth, fortune, social position, favorable opportunities, the openings which present themselves, and which seem to be manifestations of Providence, — such are the most notable indications by which, with any sort of certainty, the vocation of a young man becomes revealed. By observing these indications, by following them with prudent circumspection, we shall very rarely be deceived; if we are sometimes deceived, which hardly ever occurs, it is in cases where the error cannot be serious, because the differences will be of trifling importance, and the vocation less obligatory. But parents or teachers must not, in this respect, violently urge children with respect to this. Their liberty ought to be respected. They can, they ought to enlighten, and betimes prepare and direct them; but to urge and drive them by compulsion into such or such a state, never!

As to the more perfect and supernatural vocations, I shall speak of them somewhat in detail in a forthcoming work, when I shall treat of the liberty of ecclesiastical vocations, and the respect due to them. At present, I shall confine myself to saying simply this, Without doubt, every one in this world can, with the assistance of God, raise himself to great eminence. The sphere of truth and virtue, like that of goodness and divine grace, is immense; and there is for each, in the designs of Providence, a degree of relative perfection, which it is permissible for him to attain; this is what we may with St. Paul call, *Voluntas Dei bene placens et perfecta.* But, alas! how few succeed in it! many degenerate. For these latter, God, in His mercy, may reserve vocations less perfect, and a future less high, but which can always be good and generous if they be faithful. It is still life and salvation. But there are some who fall below all limits and the entire will of God; these are they who desire to do nothing in this world, or who do nothing but evil, not taking any account of the laws of their Creator. For these last, it is ruin; it is intellectual and moral degradation; it is eternal death: *Ad nihilum redactus est in conspectu ejus malignus.* But whatever may be the latitude permitted to each in the choice of the various vocations possible, it is manifest that this choice, blind or enlightened, happy or unfortunate, conformable or contrary to the order of Providence, will have a singular influence on the future, and make the happiness or woe, the shame or honor, of life — the glorious promise or utter failure of an entire existence. For this reason, parents ought not only not give way to their personal vanity, their ambition, the desires of self-love, but should also guard well against too lightly placing their faith in the certainty of omens which may be indifferent or premature. They must have a religious caution for the liberty of the child, leaving the good disposition to be declared by himself; the influence of grace marks out the designs of Providence; the capacities gradually reveal themselves; the talents become declared and certain; in a word, they should study attentively the order of Nature and Providence, in order to obey it. Truth strangely forgotten in our days, when the greater number of vocations and professions are decided at random, and without any serious examination; when we see children who seem to be, by the most manifest indications of Providence, called one day to govern their country, or, at least, to fill the most important civil or political posts in it, brought up, permit me to say, as if they were one day to be only painters or musicians, or even, to descend still lower, huntsmen or grooms. The most remarkable among them draws, if you will, or sings more or less agreeably; they will say he is a distinguished man! What will he have performed during his life? perhaps filled an album! Again, the greater number will know only how to dance, fence, and ride.

> "Pour toute ambition, pour vertu singulière,
> Il excelle à conduire un char dans la carrière,"

Racine formerly said. How many young men of our day confine all their ambition to that; and, strange coincidence! curious contrast! in this same country we see a multitude of other children, not predestined, either by the wish of Nature or the call of Providence, to rise in any way above the crowd, and who, imprudently brought up to a kind of life for which God has not intended them, contract, in the theatre of a false education, tastes, luxurious habits, immoderate wants, which prepare for their whole life the uneasiness and torments of an ambition which it will one day be necessary to satisfy, perhaps, at any price. Frightful error! which, by its consequences, hollows beforehand in the path of the man an abyss of crime or despair, and almost always both! What, also, frequently comes to pass? While the first, citizens without worth, fathers of families without righteousness, are not capable of bringing up their children nor managing their property, and originate or hasten the decay by which names, illustrious during a long period, are going at last to be extinguished in obscurity, and sometimes in ignominy; the second produce those envioüs, turbulent, factious generations, to whom, in spite of their mediocrity, all wealth, all social superiority, is a hateful spectacle, an insupportable burden; unhappy men, who, in the bitter vexation of their rebellious pride, raise disturbances in the bosom of society, in order to spring violently above their condition, and, tormented by dreams of unmeasured cupidity, at length find repose only in their own ruin, or the overthrow of public order. Which are the most culpable? Certainly the question is of trifling importance; but, if it be my duty to solve it, I will say, Those for whom God and society had done so much, and who do not wish to do anything for Him, for themselves, or for it; who retain no remembrance of their name, their ancestors, or their past glory; who destroy in themselves the brightest hopes of the country, and so many valuable gifts, which perhaps will never be found again; in fine, who allow the most elevated and priceless powers of a great nation to become enervated and swallowed up by the effeminacy and indolence of their lives; I will say, these latter irritate me more profoundly, discourage, dishearten me; these latter would cause me to despair of the future, if it were not for Providence, the moral influence of the Church, and the destiny of France. Excuse the bitterness of my grief and my words; and, in order to justify them, permit me to make a more general reflection, which, I trust, will not appear too harsh;. I protest I do not at least intend it to be so; it is a simple matter of fact, which every one will find within the limits of his own experience, and which will one day throw a new light on the thesis I now maintain, respecting the importance of a state, or some vocation whatsoever, for each individual, and the danger of false or defective vocations. When one has studied human nature in the child, that is to say, from its starting-point, and followed it through the different ages of man, even to the extreme confines of life, he is struck by the number of rich, intelligent, ardent, brilliant, honest, and virtuous natures stopped short in their flight, cramped in their energy, obscured in their brilliancy, not displaying what they have received, and only leaving it to be divined by its flashes; abortive intellects, unworthy of themselves; paralyzed, contracted hearts; noble creatures, whom an impoverished sap, turned from its course, has rendered apathetic, incomplete, sterile; carrying off the most beautiful hopes of religion, home, and society, and making shipwreck of the high destiny which God had prepared for them. From whence arises this misfortune? Most frequently from a false, a defective vocation. These are the people who have, or wish to have, nothing to do in this world, which is the most serious of disorders, and the greatest of dangers; or those who, not having studied either their own character or the designs of Providence, have wished to do what was not intended for them. Alas! I speak with too much experience of this; and I fear, during some moments, and against my will, a sorrowful emotion, which is not bitterness, but the too justifiable accents of a devotion frequently betrayed in its holiest and dearest aspirations! What thoughtless parents! What rash and hasty decisions in the most serious business of life! How many young people, even, have I not seen called upon to decide their own destiny, deluding themselves most strangely, and, by a blind choice, binding their intellect and their will to a profession for which they were not prepared themselves, giving and stamping with frightful levity a wrong direction to their life, in an age of passion and inexperience; fixing the limits of their virtue, and acting the same part even towards their religion!

On all sides, also, how many erring vocations and misplaced existences! how many disappointments! how many minds led astray, characters lessened, virtues compromised, services and hopes destroyed! And these young people become men, old men, such as they are brought up; for the child becomes the young man, the young man the mature man, the mature man the old man; in fine, all form society, this society which has many rules, but no resources, against the greater number of the evils which devour it, and which has neither laws nor remedies against these evils. I deceive myself; not only has society neither laws nor remedies against such evils, but, strange to say, it has laws to create them, laws to hallow them, laws against the remedies for these evils.

CONCLUSION.

THEN — for it is time we should sum up all this book and these details — to form man, and prepare him for the various social offices he will one day be called to fill on earth; to form man by this general education, which may be suitably called the perfection of human education; to form him by an education suitable to the vocation Providence assigns to him, his social position, his talents, and his particular tastes; to form man, — that is to say, this noble creature, gifted with intelligence, reason, and free-will, created for happiness; to form man, intelligent, upright man, with his ordinary faculties and his individual qualities, such as society and religion require him; man, above all, with a pure and powerful intellect in a vigorous and healthy body — *mens sana in corpore sano;* the man of sense, judgment, and taste; the man of heart, the man of character; the man of disciplined mind, of easy and clear utterance; the man of firm and upright will, according to the degree of sense, imagination, character, or genius, which is the stamp of his individuality; the man of enlightened faith and confirmed conscience; man such as God has created him, and as Jesus Christ has regenerated him; man such as the providential progress of the world has perfected him; the man of his age and his country, in accordance with the wisest and happiest meaning of these two words; in fine, the Christian, for this name includes all; and we do not fulfil our high mission if we do not know how to form Christian hearts, and bring up, in accordance with Christianity, and even the Gospel, those whom society confides to us.

Such, then, is the work education ought to accomplish, and it is by that it will form men for society without endangering it or them, and that it will have the power of producing, in every step of the social hierarchy, men perfected according to the means and extent suitable to each, in order to exalt them to eternal life. We shall now ask, Have we exaggerated in any way by saying education is a divine work, and in giving to it so high and decisive an importance with respect to the dignity and happiness of individuals, families, and all society? I understand that such a theory may be exposed to meet with more than one astonished or even incredulous smile in an age which, to the present day, seems, at least, hardly to understand the dignity of education, and which, perhaps, will consider what we speak of as an absurd theory, and a speculation impossible to be realized in practice. Well, no; permit me to express frankly all my ideas here. No, it is not an absurd theory; for it is by converting this theory into practice, all Europe has been elevated to the highest civilization; and if France has, during a long period, kept her place at the head of modern nations — queen of civilized Europe — it is to this fine and vigorous education she owes this glory. No, it is not a foolish theory, a speculation impossible to be realized. I willingly cry out, Shame and woe to the teachers of youth who could look on it thus! If there exist, and there will, even to the end of this sad world, a creature really worthy of the elevation of this theory, and the respect which it professes for the greatness of his origin, and if the practice of it were impossible, he should despair of humanity, of his country, of his family, of himself; in fine, of God and His Providence. Teachers of youth, who do not yet, perhaps, understand these matters, guard yourselves from receiving them with a silly and haughty disdain. Are you, then, ignorant of what is in question here, and what interests are confided to you? It is human nature, it is man and his offspring; they are the children of God who are remitted to your care. No, no, it is not a speculation impossible to be realized! While there shall still remain on earth a creature of this race, of whom God has said, "Let us make man to our own image and likeness," the education of man will be the grandest of works, a providential and sacred labor, a task entirely divine, a priesthood. While there shall remain on earth intelligences which God has created, capable of knowledge and wisdom, capable of truth and light, capable of thought and memory, capable of science and genius, it will be beautiful, it will be praiseworthy, it will be divine, to labor for the education, the intellectual elevation, of such noble creatures. While there shall remain on earth a heart, a conscience, a character, a human will, it will be beautiful, it will be praiseworthy, it will be divine, to mould them to the love of what is true and upright, to enthusiasm for what is noble, elevated, generous, to a holy passion for what is great and sublime. Yes, while there shall remain on earth a son of man inspired by this divine breath, which makes him the king of creation, and the immortal image of the living God, he should be brought up in the knowledge and love of his high destiny, and, in order to do that, established by this high education, the theory of which surprises you, in the integrity, the strength, the plenitude, and the power of his incomparable faculties. While there shall remain on earth one of those whom God has visibly created in order to become, by science and the love of natural and supernatural objects, the centre of creation, and to contemplate the heavens, it will be beautiful to teach him by what efforts, by what studies, by what intellectual, moral, and religious elevation, he ought to render himself superior to all that which God has submitted to his eyes and the investigations of his intellect; it will be beautiful to teach him by what admirable ways he can attain, from the insignificant point he occupies on earth, to everything, even to the extremity of his empire; study the most sublime mysteries of nature; measure with certainty the immensity of the heavens; penetrate even to the bowels of the earth; and, by discovering its treasures, contemplate all, from the grass and the flowers of the field, which live but a day, and, before dying, humbly reveal to him their names, their species, their properties, and their virtues, even to the sun, which is the measure of centuries, and by which he can follow with his eye, in the vast spaces of the firmament, the path that this planet itself blindly traverses. While there shall remain a son of man on earth, it will be beautiful, it will be praiseworthy, to teach him, above all, that it is by the noble alliance of knowledge with virtue, of literature with wisdom, of science with faith, of arts with religion, he can succeed in cultivating his faculties to the highest power of genius; to this power, by which the mind of man with a single thought embraces the universe, places himself on its ultimate limits, and, without becoming pale, looks beyond; to this power of an almost divine activity, which bounds to the heights of the heavens, and descends again with rapidity to the depths of the abysses; which, by the powerful glance of history, embraces and rules every century, contemplates and judges the present century, which is the measure of his passing existence, and plunges without terror into the centuries of an unbounded future. While there shall remain on earth any of these souls whom God has created so great, and that they should not, when arriving even at the extreme limits of time, despair either of themselves, or of the times, or of the world which completes and breaks up behind them, it will be praiseworthy, it will be beautiful, it will be divine — divine to teach them with what faith, with what hope, they should magnanimously spring into eternity. And, in fine, if a bishop may be permitted to proclaim the height to which Christian education should raise itself, we say that it is to that of revealing to those whom it brings up, even during their early years, how Christians, fallen from heaven, can find again the road to it with certainty, and laboriously re-conquer the glory of it. It is, then, for Christian education to teach its disciples gradually that the entire world is nothing; that they ought to know how to despise the earth; and that, the farther they advance in life, the more they will find of narrowness and evil in those inferior regions which hold them captive; and that if they desire to satiate the thirst for happiness which lies deep in their nature, and the intense eagerness of their souls, it is at the foot of the altars of evangelical grace that they will find wings in order to fly far, very far, away from that which is for them but a disgraced and blighted kingdom, even into the invisible regions, where they can, with a real right, aspire to possess God Himself, and become united with Him in the splendors and delights of eternity. But if some men of the present age still find this speculation too elevated, permit me to tell them it is because they have remained too long disciples of that eighteenth century, the impious levity of which despised human dignity, at least as much as it outraged Divine Majesty, and whose theories of education were so profoundly subversive of all social and religious order, of all authority, and of all respect. But the rising generation repels far from it the abject doctrines and teachings of this gross philosophy. I have profound confidence in it; generous understandings will not be wanting among us, elevated minds, for whom this beautiful theory will not be absurd, nor this high speculation impossible to realize, and, in a word, who understand what a child is, and the respect due to the dignity of his nature.

www.ingramcontent.com/pod-product-compliance
Lightning Source LLC
LaVergne TN
LVHW010214110826
845151LV00004B/1080

* 9 7 8 1 4 2 5 5 2 8 2 8 7 *